Memorable Moments Of A Met Copper

1967–1997

David Dugmore

Published by

MELROSE BOOKS

An Imprint of Melrose Press Limited
St Thomas Place, Ely
Cambridgeshire
CB7 4GG, UK
www.melrosebooks.co.uk

FIRST EDITION

Cover designed by Melrose Books

ISBN   978-1-912026-68-5
epub   978-1-912026-69-2
mobi   978-1-912026-70-8

Printed and bound in Great Britain by:
Print2Demand Ltd
24 Enterprise House
Silsoe
Bedfordshire
MK45 4HS

CONTENTS

PREFACE

For reasons that will become evident as you progress through this book, I currently have an unprecedented amount of spare time on my hands — not an ideal position for me to be in at this stage in my life. Without something constructive and meaningful to occupy my mind, I would quickly go stir-crazy and demented out of boredom, leaving the way open to whatever mischief I could devise!

My daughters quickly identified my dilemma and did their utmost to convince me that a good way of channelling my mental dexterity and keep me busy would be for me to put down in print my past police experiences. They thought these would be of interest to a broad section of the public and not just my immediate family. At first, I dismissed their suggestion, as I was reluctant to believe that there was any substance to it. In fact, I thought that they were simply trying to bolster my flagging self-belief. Furthermore, I have had no formal training or guidance in writing or presenting any form of literature, and I have no contacts in connection with the publication of such material.

I soon realised that with modern electronic equipment, such as computers, together with the various methods of social media, Facebook and Twitter for example, which are readily accessible to all and sundry, a lot of my concerns are now obsolete and redundant. Without wishing to sound arrogant, the more my daughters attempted to entice me into completing this project, the more I became aware that I could possibly recall some significant experiences from my work in the police service that some people might find compulsive reading. It is largely down to my daughters' efforts, their perseverance and their persuasiveness that I finally decided to complete this project. As the saying goes, 'the proof is in the pudding'; only time will tell whether or not I have succeeded. While I doubt I will be around to see the results of my labour, I wish it well. However, some solace can be taken from the fact that, if nothing else has been achieved, these memoirs have enabled me to retain my sanity!

DEDICATION

This compilation of memories and experiences, which are recorded in a chronological sequence for ease of reference, are dedicated to all those people I have interacted with during my police service who have influenced my development as a human being. However, more importantly, these memoirs have been prepared in recognition of the deep devotion, gratitude and respect I have for my wonderful soulmate and wife, Paula, who was taken from me so tragically and prematurely in June 2008 at the age of 60 following a brief illness. Her most remarkable attribute was her unwavering ability to consistently consider others before herself. I rarely see this selfless trait exhibited in members of the younger generation in modern society, as they tend to be more self-centred and less community orientated.

I also wish to recognise the significant contributions my children have made in recent months towards my general well-being at a very difficult and problematic juncture in my life. Having had to contend with the knowledge that I have contracted a pervasive form of cancer, which will leave me with an uncertain future, their support and assistance has helped me to maintain a positive and progressive outlook, instead of burying myself in a state of mental denial. Accordingly, I made a conscious decision to ignore anything not relevant at present and to only deal with issues that may become pertinent in the future. I simply concentrate all my energy on matters that enhance my independence and quality of life. The enthusiasm and encouragement exhibited by my children stimulated my interest in recounting some of the more unusual, bizarre and stimulating situations I faced during my police career. Albeit, motivating me to complete this project was more challenging. Apart from a basic lack of confidence in my ability to express myself satisfactorily in print, I also normally prefer to keep matters relating to personal recollections and emotions to myself and private. Experience has taught me that broadcasting to a wider audience can and does, on occasion, lead to distortion and misunderstanding. In this case, I am satisfied that common sense and perseverance has prevailed. Congratulations, kids.

PERSONAL PROFILE

Whatever path the rest of my life takes, I would be the first to acknowledge that I have been lucky enough to have led a full, constructive and productive life, with a significant amount of contentment thrown in for good measure. Without doubt, my solid and well-balanced childhood assisted my development into adulthood which, I believe, enabled me to make a small, yet valid, contribution to society at large. While my childhood could be regarded as different from the norm, it was, in my opinion, far from privileged. To the contrary, there were elements to it that were distinctly disadvantageous to youngsters residing in a permanent single location throughout their childhood.

I was born on the 27th May 1948 on the island of St. Vincent in the Cape Verdes, the eldest of three children, two boys and a girl, to parents who many people would regard, even in this 'politically correct' society we now live in, as 'middle class'. However, I would argue that such a tag would be both inaccurate and misleading, as my parents actually came from sound 'working stock' who, through hard work and determination, managed to better themselves. While their financial resources were constantly limited throughout my childhood, my parents were always conscious of the needs of their children and endeavoured to respond accordingly. I can't remember ever having to go without something, although second-hand products and hand-me-downs often had to suffice. They were a loving, caring and considerate couple who instilled in us high moral standards, ethics and principles. Failing to meet these standards would normally be followed by a mild form of 'corporal' punishment — a single smack to the calf or thigh. Such an action generally had the desired effect of preventing a repeat of the misbehaviour. Punishment was always administered in a firm but fair manner, with an equal measure of debate and praise as necessary. This balance ensured that no throwbacks, either physiological or psychological, were taken into later adult life. I am confident that my own children, who were raised in a similar way, would concur with my sentiments. Consequently, I find today's 'namby-pamby' approach to physical admonishment of children to be completely incomprehensible. I may well be missing some fundamental concept, but I fail to see what is to be gained by simply trying to reason, rationalise or negotiate with the perpetrators of bad or unsociable behaviour; an adequate deterrent is usually the only real way to guarantee compliance.

One distinct advantage I had over the majority of my peers from my generation was the extensive foreign travel I experienced during my formative years. My father, an electrical engineer, was on the foreign staff of the large British communications company, Cable and Wireless. He was sent on postings abroad that would last from 18 months to three years, depending on the location, climate and state of development of the respective country. In addition to St. Vincent, up until the age of 17, I lived in a number of countries around the world, including Ceylon (now Sri Lanka), Brazil, Gibraltar, Ghana (West Africa), Sierra Leone (West Africa), Madeira and Malta (twice). Clearly, this type of lifestyle broadened my outlook on life by providing me with a greater insight into global problems and practical issues. However, while enhancing my knowledge in areas such as economics, politics, religion and industry, it failed to address many of the basic subjects associated with a normal education. The quality and consistency of education abroad was often poor and, on occasion, non-existent.

At 10 years of age, I left my parents in Gibraltar and returned to England alone, where I stayed with my grandparents prior to starting my first of six years at boarding school. Of the three schools I attended, Harlow College in Old Harlow, Essex, was the main seat of my education. It was quickly established that, while I was a gifted sportsman who excelled at a number of different games, including cricket, badminton and squash, I was not the brightest light on the block academically. A poor short-term memory, coupled with mild dyslexia, meant study was always a difficult and rather unpleasant task, requiring hard work and commitment. In June 1965, I re-joined my parents, who were then on their second tour of Malta. From that time until September 1966, I attended the Royal Naval College, Tal Handaq, where I completed my schooling and managed to gain a number of good qualifications, exceeding even my own expectations. Aside from sheer stubbornness on my part, I have much to thank my father for, as his help was invaluable in passing my exams.

After leaving college in August 1966, I returned to the United Kingdom where I joined the 'A' level managerial scheme at Sainsbury's Ltd., working at the Romford and Collier Row branches. Irrespective of having reached the exalted position of 'senior leading salesman' in next to no time, I quickly became bored and disillusioned with the lack of variety in my work and the rather mundane routine involved in its completion. An early opportunity to change the direction of my career presented itself one morning when I saw the centrefold of the national newspaper I was reading. It was a double-page advertisement seeking recruits to join the Metropolitan Police Force (now Service or M.P.S.). On an impulse, I submitted an application form to become a police constable. Within two months, I had been interviewed and selected for the position, and on the 27th November 1967, I commenced my basic police training and probationary period and I haven't looked back since! As will be seen later in this memoir, the M.P.S. offered a wide selection of work choices, together with commensurate variety which, in the main, were interesting, absorbing and challenging. The Service also offered good prospects for advancement and specialisation. In addition to attaining the rank of chief superintendent prior to my retirement in November 1997, I had also undertaken a number of 'operational and supervisory' courses in my chosen specialist subject

— that of 'public order'. The expertise gained in this field undoubtedly placed me in the front line of many more hazardous situations and in harm's way more frequently than many of my colleagues.

While my police pension was more than adequate to provide Paula and myself with a good standard of living without having to seek further full- or part-time employment, I felt that, at the age of 50, I was far too young to retire and simply sit back, twiddle my fingers and watch the world pass by. As an active individual, both mentally and physically, I realised that vegetating was not a rational or realistic option. Clearly, I needed something constructive into which to channel all my energies. At the same time, I was conscious that, as a senior supervisor of a large workforce for many years, the prospect of working for an organisation where a number of 'pimply-faced' young employees could have power and authority over me, was not a particularly appealing prospect. Not wishing to continue in the fields of law and security upon my retirement, in respect of which most of my professional knowledge and skills were honed, I realised my options were limited. Accordingly, my desire to do something completely different and independent with my working life, had to be tempered by the knowledge that I needed to find an outlet where I could use and consolidate other attributes I had gained during my police service.

In early 1998, with my advanced driving qualifications, security-clearance level and proven business acumen in support, I presented before my Local Authority, Brentwood District Council, an application seeking a 'private hire operator's licence'. Such a licence would enable me to run my own 'up-market' private taxi service. However, my application was unprecedented and highly irregular, as consideration, up until that time, had only ever been given to applicants who had held a taxi driver's licence and had already been driving for an independent 'operator' for at least two years. Although granting me an 'operator' licence would set a precedent, it was eventually approved after much heated debate amongst the 12 local councillors who formed the committee considering various public submissions that day. My business, which I ran from my home address, thrived and prospered over the next four and a half years. Owing to its growth and success, I was eventually forced into a position where I had to make a crucial decision: do I expand my business by going 'high street', with all the accompanying responsibilities and aggravation, or retire from the working rat race once and for all? With Paula's full agreement, it was decided that retirement was the most rational and sensible option. Having managed to finalise all my business interests and entered into negotiations to purchase a new property by the end of the spring of 2002, we wasted no time moving to our new home in Downham Market, Norfolk, lock, stock and barrel on the 20th June 2002.

It is now imperative that I briefly go back in time to reflect on a Police Section House dance one evening in mid-November 1969. It was, indisputably, one of the best and most influential times in my life, as it was the day when I first met my then future wife, Pauline, better known to family and friends as Paula. At the outset, I doubted our relationship would get off the ground, as within a fortnight of meeting her I was set to be seconded to Anguilla in the West Indies for a three-month posting. I'm not sure how, but we did survive this separation and grew closer together in a very short space of time. Our relationship did come under a brief period of strain in mid-1970, because Paula was living in rented accommodation near Harrods in Knightsbridge, while I was residing in police bachelor quarters in Stoke Newington, North London. The distance between us, coupled with work commitments, did not facilitate getting together on a regular basis. This bumpy time was resolved expeditiously when Paula, together with a friend who also worked as a member of the civil staff at New Scotland Yard, rented a flat in Tottenham, North London. While the area was suffering from social deprivation and housing neglect, it was very close to where I was living and it wasn't long before we were cohabiting.

Irrespective of the fact that Paula was basically a shy and retiring person, whereas I was a more outgoing, gregarious and stubborn individual, we found that our likes, dislikes, aspirations and ambitions were virtually identical. Our differences in personality only served to bond us together more tightly, albeit it didn't prevent us from having some monumental rows during our happy 36-year marriage; making-up was such great fun though! It would probably be an understatement to say that I couldn't have wished for a more loyal best friend, great lover and companion than Paula. We finally tied the knot and got married on 24 June 1972, when we moved into police married quarters in Cannonbury, Islington, North London. After two years, we bought our first property in Rainham, Essex and subsequently moved twice more before I retired to Pilgrims Hatch and Ingrave, within the area of Brentwood, Essex. The only real regret I have in the twilight of my life, is the feeling of total desolation and abandonment over Paula's untimely and unfair death in circumstances which were so out of character. I'm not bitter, just saddened. However, having been taken from me far too early, when she was only 60 years young, my anger and frustration will never be quenched and will remain with me for the rest of my days.

On top of a remarkable marriage, I am also blessed with three fantastic children, Danielle, Dominique and Damien. While none are perfect (but who is?), they never gave us sleepless nights or any significant problems. Although quite different in many ways, each of them gained good academic qualifications, secured highly responsible and respectable jobs and are leading productive lives. While I accept that I could be accused of bias, I can say with some conviction that each of my children has grown into a responsible, caring and considerate adult. I am immensely proud of all their achievements and love them more than words can express. Well, at least Paula and I must have done something right with their upbringing!

POTTED SERVICE HISTORY

I joined the Metropolitan Police Service on the 27th November 1967 and retired from it thirty years and three days later on Sunday 30th November 1997. It would be fair to say that during my service, I saw and experienced many things in life, both good and bad. Regrettably, the latter predominated, but I suppose that was the nature of the beast, bearing in mind my particular profession. Fortunately, most people can avoid dealing with life in its raw state, where their basic instincts and inhumanity to each other are so transparent.

I was enrolled and sworn into the M.P.S. upon my arrival at the residential training school Peel House at Regency Street, Victoria, SW1. I was billeted in one of the dormitories on the 3rd floor of this five-story building, in a small and pretty unsubstantial box room constructed of thin wooden partitions. Each dormitory contained a number of these self-contained living quarters, better known to the recruits as 'horse boxes', which were sparsely furnished with a single bed, small desk and chair and a cupboard for clothing.

This initial course, which lasted a total of 13 weeks, was very intensive and exceedingly demanding, both mentally and physically. It incorporated learning many aspects of statute and common law, much of which had to be learnt by 'rote'. This was then followed by practical exercises to ensure the students had clearly understood the meaning behind what they had studied and were not simply repeating phrases like a parrot. At various stages during our training, recruits were required to sit written examinations. Anyone failing to pass would be held back from progressing to the next stage with their colleagues. They would be dropped down a class and given another opportunity to take the same exam a week or so later. Failure on a second occasion was met with instant dismissal from the training school and the M.P.S. Your confirmation as a 'probationary constable' was solely dependent on passing the final written examination, as a consequence of which your status was not announced until you were in your final week of training.

While attending this initial training course, strict rules and discipline were imposed and enforced. Breaches or failure to comply were met with pretty harsh punishments such as detentions, early morning parades, additional gym work and the removal of certain personal privileges. Because of the strict regime, intensive study requirements and limited availability of facilities within the establishment, students were permitted to venture out of the school in 'mufty' (civilian clothing) and enjoy the many attractions Central London had to offer at the conclusion of classes each day. However, a 10pm curfew was in force and although there was no formal roll call or checking procedure in operation, anyone caught by a member of staff returning after curfew would instantly be placed on report and punished. As will be seen later in this memoir, there was only one effective way to escape detection, but this also had some unpleasant consequences.

All those of us who had managed to pass our final examination at the first time of asking were shepherded into the gymnasium during our final, thirteenth week of training, when our first operational posting was announced. I was being sent to Old Street / City Road sub-division, which formed part of Hackney Division within 'G' District. This division was renowned to be a very difficult and demanding area to police. It was suffering from racial tension, particularly from within the West Indian community, poverty, social deprivation, poor housing and consistently high levels of crime. Irrespective of all these negative factors, I can only remember that in my innocent enthusiasm, and with the wealth of knowledge I had acquired, which I wanted to put into practice, I just wanted to get 'out and at 'em' as soon as possible.

I was finally released onto the unsuspecting public of Hackney in early March 1968.

Soon after being posted to Hackney Division, I was thrust into a baptism of fire when I was placed in the front line of the defensive police cordon outside the American Embassy during the Grosvenor Square riot, but more about that incident later, save to say, it was a very frightening and intimidating situation. Late in 1969, while still a young and raw uniform constable, I was seconded to the Anguilla Police Unit in the Caribbean, in company with members from the army's Royal Engineers, to protect the local population against a threatened invasion by forces from the neighbouring island of St. Kitts. As will be seen from references I make to this tour of duty later in this manuscript, my time on Anguilla was more like an extremely enjoyable holiday than work. The local inhabitants were very welcoming and hospitable and there was no hint of hostility from any quarter.

Having taken and passed two competitive examinations, a number of promotion selection board interviews and various residential management courses, I worked through the 'uniform' rank structure until I reached the position of divisional commander. During my career in the M.P.S., I served almost exclusively in the East End of London, with brief excursions to the West End and New Scotland Yard. Looking back, it seems that I had the habit of going from the proverbial frying pan into the fire!

On being promoted to sergeant in 1972, I was transferred to Albany Street/Tottenham Court Road Police Stations, which were part of 'E' District. While on the fringe of the business hub of Central London, the area will best be remembered for its varied and plentiful 'night' activity amongst the many seedy/sleazy clubs and bars. Frequented by tourists visiting the capital and local residents, predominantly members from the Irish labourer community, a high demand for police services and their regular deployment could be guaranteed.

During the five years I worked on Albany Street Division ('ED'),

I spent almost three of them in plain clothes, in charge of the local 'vice squad', working on undercover operations. I developed an expertise in connection with illegal gaming, the majority of which related to Greek card games of chance, pornography, the illegal sale of alcohol, drugs dealing and prostitution. Prostitution was divided into two quite distinct, but separate, categories. Part of the work involved arresting and bringing to justice those men who controlled and lived off prostitutes who frequented and plied their trade in and around Kings Cross and St Pancras railway stations, better known as 'pimps' or 'ponces'. The other element of the 'live' sex industry I concentrated on related to sauna parlours that offered considerably more than a £5 rub down with an oily rag! Bearing in mind that maintaining my anonymity was paramount when performing plain-clothes duties, I had to look and play the part of those living in a subterranean and often squalid level of society. Consequently, when drug dealers, prostitutes or others engaged in criminal activities propositioned me, believing me to be a normal 'punter', their antics when confronted or arrested often proved to be quite comical.

On completion of this period in my service in 1977, I was placed on a temporary secondment to the Criminal Investigation Bureau (C.I.B.) at New Scotland Yard as a detective sergeant. This branch of the Service deals with allegations of internal impropriety and serious criminal offences involving police officers. I was selected to join C.I.B. as a member of a small dedicated team, to deal specifically with a major investigation into the recycling of a large quantity of drugs by police back into society at large. At the conclusion of this very complex and thorough investigation, which took almost 18 months to complete, a number of officers of different rank from the Detective Department were successfully prosecuted and sentenced to imprisonment. While attached to this department, I sat and passed the inspector's promotion examination and on promotion to that rank in 1978, I returned to the uniform branch and was posted to 'K' District within the London

Borough of Havering.

While serving in the Borough of Havering between 1979–1981, I worked as a uniform relief inspector and unit commander at Romford, Rainham and Upminster Police Stations. The single most prominent thing etched into my memory of this time, was the sheer volume of fatal road traffic accidents I was called upon to deal with personally; a total of 24 in little more than 18 months. Of the many tasks and functions I had to perform during my service, the most arduous, sensitive, emotional and difficult to fulfil was, without doubt, notifying parents of the death of a child. Irrespective of my ability as a good communicator, I never found an easy way to break such devastating news. On every occasion I had to impart such tidings, I found it heartbreaking watching the facial expressions of the families as their worlds fell apart.

Now I come to that phase in my career, 1983–1991, when I performed a number of roles at different ranks at a variety of locations over a relatively short period of time. Initially, I returned to a department at New Scotland Yard, known as A2 Branch, which had responsibility for producing and publishing Service policy issues and procedures. My work during this period was largely administrative and uneventful. In 1984, I was posted back to 'G' District as the operations chief inspector for Hackney Division. Sadly, I was the late duty senior officer on the day of the Tottenham riots and, as explained later, I was present at this disastrous event, with responsibilities that left me with some mental scars.

During 1985–1986, whilst still officially attached to Hackney Division, I spent the majority of my duty time, on average 12 hours a day for an entire year, policing the Wapping print dispute. On alternate weeks, I would perform the role of 'controller', with responsibility for the implementation of police tactics/strategy and the deployment of resources, and actually taking operational command of a sector within the area of the demonstration. This was yet another rather unpleasant phase during my career, when my officers and I came under repeated unprovoked attacks from concrete slabs, wooden poles used as spears, and even torn up lamp posts. I have to say that, although most print workers were decent people, there was a vociferous minority from 'rent a crowd', who had little or no connection with that industry, who were present simply to orchestrate disorder and violence, usually from a safe distance from the seat of any trouble. When the Wapping dispute was finally resolved, I returned to my operational duties at Hackney Police Station, which included a clap down on premises selling unlicensed liquor.

When I was promoted to superintendent in 1988, I was selected by my local assistant commissioner to perform the role of community liaison officer for the London Borough of Hackney, based at Stoke Newington Police Station. Albeit very exacting, the post proved to be extremely interesting and rewarding, requiring no small measure of political dexterity and diplomacy, together with some knowledge about ethnic cultures and religions. Much of my work involved building bridges between the Afro-Caribbean and Asian communities, where basic mistrust of authority had been endemic for generations. Without wishing to sound too smug and self-righteous, I believe that by the time I left this post I had made positive progress and a valid contribution towards improving police/public relations. Good rapport was established between many sections of the community and I had managed to introduce a number of innovative ideas with shared responsibility.

In 1991, after having served a total of over 12 years in the Borough of Hackney, I thought it was about time to have a complete change of working environment. Accordingly, I applied for a transfer from the most deprived borough in Europe to the second most deprived, that of Newham. My application was approved and I took up a vacancy as deputy divisional commander at Plaistow Division 'KO'. In addition to the normal duties associated with my post, I also had responsibility for the planning and implementation of police arrangements connected with the football Premiership club, West Ham United. When I first arrived, we were plagued by hooliganism, but this was slowly and resolutely eradicated during the five seasons I was associated with West Ham football. While every community has a criminal fraternity, it normally only amounts to a relatively small percentage of its overall population. I doubt I would be contradicted when I say that the undesirable element within Newham is probably significantly higher than elsewhere in the U.K. Upon the retirement of my immediate superior in 1994, I took over the role of divisional commander with the rank of A/ chief superintendent.

At the beginning of 1996, I was given what would prove to be my last operational posting before my retirement from the Service in November 1997. I was promoted to operations command unit manager for '2 Area Operations'. The 400-plus staff, both civilian and police, who came under my direct command were split into four distinct groups; Dog Section, Mounted Branch, Traffic Patrol and Territorial Support Group (shield trained personnel). While engaged in this post, I was embroiled in the carnage and destruction caused by the I.R.A. Docklands bomb. As the senior police officer in situ, I had overall command over the emergency services in attendance and responsibility for co-ordinating the subsequent assistance provided for the clear-up operation.

Regrettably, my retirement from the M.P.S., which should have been a time for celebration, was overshadowed by the murder of one of my young woman police officers named Nina McKay, who was attached to the Territorial Support Group. She was stabbed to death by a psychopath as she entered his premises with her colleagues under the authority of an arrest warrant. To make matters worse, the media presented a somewhat distorted picture of events, by inferring that she was not wearing appropriate protective equipment; this assertion is completely inaccurate. Apart from being a member of my team,

I knew her family well. Her father, a retired Metropolitan Police chief superintendent, had been my supervising sergeant many years earlier when I was still a 'green horn' bobby. After her death, it fell to me to ensure that all the necessary arrangements were in place for her 'Service' funeral. Having two daughters of my own, this incident was a poignant reminder of our frailty as human beings and the need to cherish every moment we have together with our families, as we never know what might be lurking around the next corner!

MEMORABLE MOMENTS

Having racked my brain, I have managed to recall a number of specific incidents/events which I personally experienced during my police service and which I consider 'stand out in the crowd'. They represent a broad spectrum of subject matter and are not restricted solely to practical policing issues. It is hoped the reader finds the following examples thoroughly absorbing, unusual, compelling, thought provoking and interesting. Although many of my recollections are humorous and quite light-hearted, others are very serious and upsetting, with dire consequences. Why should I have so many brutal and frightening memories? Well, the answer to this question lies in the fact that, owing to the numerous operational and supervisory courses I undertook in the field of 'public order', I obtained a higher level of expertise and skill than many of my peers and contemporaries.

POLICE TRAINING SCHOOL, PEEL HOUSE – November 1967

One of the stringent rules enforced at the training school was a 10pm curfew. While there was no formal roll call or checking-in procedure in operation for students returning to the premises after an evening out, any student caught breaking this rule was immediately placed on report and punished. It quickly became common knowledge that the only certain way to avoid detection was to scramble up an external fire escape in the quadrangle, which gave access to each floor of the building via individual 'escape' windows. Unfortunately, on the top three floors, these windows led directly into student (horse box) bedrooms within communal dormitories. This method of re-entering the training school by late-night revellers became a regular occurrence but, apart from causing some sleep deprivation to the hapless recipient who occupied the room, few other problems normally arose. Most recruits appreciated their good fortune and were conscious of the saying 'But for the grace of God go I!'

One night, just before the Christmas holiday break, when it was pouring with rain and freezing cold, all hell broke loose. At about 1.30am, I, together with other students from our third-floor dormitory, were suddenly and rudely awakened from our slumbers by a commotion from the bedroom adjoining the fire escape. A group of us rushed to the room where we noticed absolute carnage had taken place: four students, who were clearly the worse for wear from alcohol, were sprawled out around the room on top of the room's occupant. The window was wide open with rain pouring in, the single bed had collapsed with its two back legs broken at their stems, muddy footprints adorned the bedclothes, a table and chair had been overturned and the floor was soaked by the outpouring of stomach contents from one or more of the unwelcome visitors.

Understandably, none of us were overly impressed with the intrusion, so we gathered up the four scoundrels who caused the disturbance and, rather unceremoniously, escorted them to the dormitory bathroom where we metered out some summary justice in the form of a 'tooth-pasting'; less ruthless than a 'feathering', but equally unpleasant and uncomfortable.

BEAT TRAINING, OLD STREET SUB DIVISION – March 1968

When joining an operational post for the first time after leaving training school, it was established practice for all new constables to be attached to a senior colleague, known as a 'parent constable', for the duration of their first four weeks on duty. This provided them with an ideal opportunity to familiarise themselves with the topography and problems of their division. Unknown to me at the time, it was also customary for a novice constable to be the butt of some pretty harmless and innocuous 'initiation' activity.

In my case, I was duped on my second day on duty. While performing late turn (2pm–10pm) at Old Street in the London Borough of Hackney, I was instructed by my partner to accompany him to a large sprawling council estate at one of the furthest parts of the sub-division, under the pretext of trying to locate a group of juveniles responsible for damaging parked motor vehicles. My 'parent' constable did a good job of giving me a false sense of security, by averting my concentration from our route through continuous conversation during our journey. On arrival, it was suggested we split up in order to cover more ground. This proved to be a ruse, as it was the last time I saw my partner that day. I had been abandoned intentionally and left to my own devices.

At this time in my career there were no 'personal' radios available with which to contact my home base or seek assistance; police vehicles were few and far between as were the fixed and solidly built 'blue' police boxes. Police 'panda' cars and other modern communications equipment had yet to be introduced as everyday issue. Accordingly, after being dumped by my partner, the only realistic way of obtaining directions back to the police station was to find one of the remote 'blue' police boxes, come across a public telephone kiosk or seek assistance from a local resident. Sod's law being what it is, it goes without saying that I did not encounter either of the former options, and I was far too embarrassed to seek guidance from a local resident for fear of being ridiculed or regarded as some sort of moron. I struggled forth on my own and eventually found my way back to Old Street Police Station, arriving shortly before I was due to book off duty. Apart from a few smirks and chuckles from constables and supervisors on my relief, no further mention was made of my absence that day. While my antics clearly provided some mild amusement and entertainment for my relief colleagues, I must admit that I failed to see the funny side of things immediately. I was physically tired after strenuously 'plodding' around the streets aimlessly, hungry from a lack of food, not having been able to take a refreshment break during my tour of duty and not a little embarrassed having got myself lost. However, I did manage to take my treatment in good spirits and this seemed to enhance my standing amongst my colleagues and acceptance as part of their extended family.

GROSVENOR SQUARE RIOT – March 1968

On the 17th March 1968, only a few days after completing my basic training, I was thrust into a baptism of fire when I was taken off late turn duty to form part of a contingent (Serial) of 2 sergeants and 20 constables from Hackney Division, to be sent to Central London in response to a demonstration being orchestrated by a man named Tariq Ali and the actress Vanessa Redgrave. As darkness closed in, the protestors, who were objecting to the Vietnam War, were becoming more hostile and vociferous as they descended on the American Embassy from 'Speakers' Corner' at Hyde Park, where they had held a rally. Contrary to subsequent assertions made by some sections of the press, that the police presence was largely made up of riot-trained officers, I can say with confidence that this suggestion was inaccurate and misleading. In fact, the vast majority of police officers who attended this demonstration were predominantly ordinary beat officers, with little or no training in public-order matters.

I can well remember, with amazing clarity, that one minute I was sitting in a warm coach parked in a side street near the embassy, talking amiably with many of my colleagues, and the next I was being jostled in the front line of the police cordon in Grosvenor Square. It was a cold miserable evening and the square was dimly lit. Standing with arms interlocked with the two constables immediately to my left and right, I looked directly at the mass of agitated humanity gathered only a few feet in front of me shouting abuse, gesticulating and generally trying to provoke a negative police response. I recollect that the protestors looked very young and dishevelled and thought that they were probably, in the main, university students and unemployed youth. Amusingly, these activists were often regarded, light heartedly, within the law enforcement fraternity, as 'rent a crowd' or 'the great unwashed'. In reality, however, they were either 'left wing' political sympathisers, dropouts from normal society, anti-establishment / authority supporters, or simply maladjusted and rebellious individuals.

Within minutes, the mood of the demonstrators deteriorated significantly and many started to poke their banners and hurl missiles at the police ranks. The scene quickly became very confusing, chaotic, frightening and extremely dangerous, with wooden poles, pieces of masonry, stones, and a variety of bottles being thrown at police officers. Those of us maintaining the police cordons were like 'cattle fodder', in that we were being attacked, seriously assaulted and wounded and the only action we were permitted to take, unless a perpetrator got close enough to be arrested, was to try and dodge the missiles heading in our direction. Without wishing to sound like a wimp, I have to admit that I was pretty scared, as I had never before seen, let alone been involved in, such a massive display of group violence and intimidation: I would have been happy to exchange my blue trousers for brown ones! Missiles were showering down on us like confetti and I saw a constable, who was standing close to me, suddenly collapse to the ground with his face badly split open after being hit by a large, empty ink bottle on the bridge of his nose.

Although I was very fortunate to emerge from this riot (for that was what it was) almost totally unscathed, I did witness a lot of my police colleagues being injured and removed from the fray. Most suffered head or facial injuries. This incident was the one and only occasion throughout my entire service, when those of us in the 'front line' were ordered to draw truncheons. Although I did not use my truncheon, I did see a few officers strike out with theirs, although I hasten to add, in self-defence. Whilst it seemed like an eternity before order was restored and the mob disbursed, it was probably little more than an hour that we had to endure the ferocious onslaught. It proved to be a long, tiring and arduous tour of duty, during which I, and many other officers, received no relief or refreshments, save for a tepid cup of tea from a mobile unit behind the embassy.

Being a young, inexperienced officer at the time of this incident, it left me quite traumatised and with negative impressions regarding some sections of society. I still find it difficult coming to terms with and understanding the reasons behind the ferocious aggression towards police that day. It appears that the activists' behaviour, which was as bad if not worse than those they were demonstrating against, had little to do with the original purpose of the demonstration. I believe that their violent hostility was nothing more than a futile attempt to express their abhorrence with authority. While I am not, and have never been, a violent man by nature, I was so upset with what I saw that day that I would have been quite happy to meter out some summary 'painful' justice to those responsible for injuring my friends and colleagues in such a callous and unprovoked manner. Most of the perpetrators were cowards, who tended to hide behind the skirts of other, more passive, demonstrators, in an effort to avoid detection and retain their anonymity.

Some of the national press portrayed the police as the aggressors and instigators of the violence. It was also suggested that the police response was generally attributed to retaliatory action. In my view, retaliation, in circumstances such as those described above, would be justifiable and should not attract unwarranted attention or criticism. So far as the police being the aggressors, such an assertion is, in my opinion, biased, inaccurate and misleading. While there may be some validity and justification to such an accusation, depending upon the reporter's political persuasion, the origin and accuracy of the information received, there is little doubt that the provocation emanated from within the ranks of the protestors. Having witnessed the course of events first hand, I would stake my reputation on the fact that the hostility, aggression, and violence was instigated, implemented and prolonged solely by people purporting to be demonstrators. That is not to say that all the police officers present responded in an equitable and appropriate manner in every instant, but it has to be recognised that their actions were driven, predominantly, on the basis of self-preservation or defence.

SLEEPING POLICEMAN – November 1968

Owing to the unpredictable nature of policing and the fact that personal communications equipment was not readily available during the early years of my career, patrolling officers were required to report in to their respective police stations at designated times during their tours of duty, to confirm their status and obtain assignments. While public telephone kiosks were used for this purpose, the static 'blue' police boxes were the regular means utilised to complete the task. These boxes were fitted with a telephone, a shelf upon which to write and a chair to sit on.

At 2am on a particularly bitter and snowy night, I was on foot patrol walking down a long road named Queensbridge Road, E. 8, towards a 'blue' police box situated about half way down. I was looking forward to entering the box and reporting in, as it would give me the opportunity to warm up for a few minutes and rest my weary feet. To my utter surprise and amazement, when I opened the door I was shrouded and almost suffocated by an acrid cloud of cigarette smoke. As this began to clear, I saw two apparently empty pint cans of Guinness beer resting on the shelf next to the phone and one of my 'elder statesman' constables slumped on the seat, snoring his heart out softly. I didn't have the heart to disturb him, or should I say I didn't have the bottle to wake him for fear of his reaction to being caught out bang to rights by a young whippersnapper. I quietly closed and locked the door and merrily made my way along my beat, where I contacted my base station using a public phone further down the road. It is interesting to note that the officer I encountered sleeping in the police box, who was coming up to retirement age, was an hour late booking off duty that night and almost prompted a search party being sent out to look for him. I would have given a week's salary to have been a fly on the wall to listen to the excuse he gave the duty inspector as to his lateness.

A MIGHTY MEATY MEETING

Following completion of the early turn parade at 6.30am at Old Street Police Station, on a pleasant Sunday morning early in April 1969, I was making my way to my designated foot patrol, when I decided to take a small detour via a cul-de-sac named Hoxton Square. This location, which was situated only a short distance (300 yards) away from the police station, had been the subject of numerous complaints from local residents concerning parking irregularities. On my arrival, I noticed that, as usual, the area was jam packed with parked motor vehicles on either side of the pavements and that there was a white mid-sized lorry stationary in the middle of the road, almost directly opposite to where I was standing, effectively blocking access and egress to the square. I saw that the tailgate of the lorry was open and that two white men in casual dress, one in his mid-thirties the other in his twenties, came from behind the lorry, each carrying a large single object over his shoulder. They went to a small utility van parked close by, where they dumped, rather unceremoniously, their loads into the back of the van. They appeared to be in a hurry and completely oblivious to what was going on around them, their concentration being focused entirely on the task at hand.

My suspicions having been aroused, I continued my stealthy approach to the front of the lorry, which was in the opposite direction to where the men were operating. As I got closer, I noticed that they were both carrying half a pig's carcass. By the time I reached the rear of the lorry, both men were back inside its storage area busy selecting their next items; their preference appeared to be full sides of bacon. Looking into the lorry, I saw that it was still more than half full of different types of meat stacked on top of each other in a number of separate piles. Both men were obviously so engrossed in their furtive

16

work that they were completely unaware of my approach or presence until I was standing directly in front of them.

Having taken them completely by surprise, their initial reactions were quite comical and their facial expressions something to behold. They dropped the sides of bacon they were carrying so quickly that I thought they had received a sudden electric shock. Both men stood before me totally dumbstruck with their mouths agape trying to look innocent. Their posture gave the impression they had wet themselves and they were squirming and fidgeting like a couple of young lads waiting to be ticked off for some minor indiscretion. The younger of the two men was the first to pluck up the courage to speak when, pointing to the stacks of meat and trying to look confident and assured, he said, "It's all real fresh, Guv, if you want some beef I can do you a good price." At this stage, his partner looked crestfallen.

No sooner had I started to ask them questions about their movements, when the older of the two men suddenly blurted out, "Okay, Guv, it's a fair cop." I was stunned momentarily as I couldn't quite believe what I had just heard. Up until that time I had considered such an expression / statement to be reserved and restricted to the entertainment industry, particularly television. In real life, I doubted anyone would have the audacity to be so forthright. After cautioning and informing them that they were being arrested, they both followed me meekly to Old Street Police Station, walking beside me and talking to me like I was a long lost friend. Once again, I was surprised by their compliance, as should they have attempted to escape from my custody there was, realistically, little I could have done to prevent them from doing so. Before departing for the police station, my 'prisoners' helped me to secure both vehicles and their contents as best as possible, pending collection by police for safe keeping and subsequent disposal to the rightful owners.

As there were no means of communicating with the police station, it was imperative that we arrived there without delay, in order to ensure the stolen meat was retrieved as soon as possible. My prisoners even accommodated me with this requirement, by walking at a fast pace. On arrival at the police station, members of the Criminal Investigation Department (C.I.D.) immediately took over responsibility for the investigation. I was later informed by the C.I.D. detective sergeant in charge of the case that my two prisoners were well known local 'villains', who were not averse to having a pop at police. I was also told that the theft of this consignment of meat represented a high value load of several thousands of pounds. I was thanked for my efforts and encouraged to apply to join the C.I.D. upon completion of my probation.

CARIBBEAN ISLAND OF ANGUILLA – 1969/1970

Early in 1969, a small group of highly charged vociferous Anguillans, led by a Mr. Ron Webster, protested vocally against Britain and its local representatives from St. Kitts, Nevis and Anguilla continuing to govern the island. They wanted independence for Anguilla and complete self-determination in administering its affairs. When their protestations fell on deaf ears, they displayed their disillusionment and frustration by taking the rather bold, yet rash, step of physically ejecting the British high commissioner for the island from his residence and then repatriating him to the U.K. at gun point. It will come as no surprise that this draconian behaviour got the full attention of the British Government, who responded immediately by dispatching a detachment of paratroopers, Royal Engineers and Metropolitan Police Officers to Anguilla to suppress any insurrection and restore law and order.

Volunteers were sought from within the M.P.S. for police officers to undertake a three-month tour of duty on the island. Although I applied for this secondment, I had little confidence that I would be selected because of my youth and the fact that, at that time, I had only just completed my police probation. Surprisingly, I was chosen and I put this down to my previous experience living with black communities in Africa. My tour of duty spanned the 1969–1970 Christmas period. Upon reflection, it would be a gross exaggeration to suggest that my attachment was remotely connected with work. During my time on Anguilla I never encountered any unpleasantness or hostility whatsoever. To the contrary, members of the local community were extremely friendly and hospitable and very supportive of our presence. From the following examples, I'm sure the consensus of opinion would be that my stay on the island was more like an extended good-quality holiday!

(A). THE LOOMING LOBSTER

I befriended one of only two local police constables who, like myself, was a keen swimmer and naturalist. Since Anguilla is a small island of about seven square miles, we managed to visit most of the pristine swimming sites around the coast during my secondment. The corals and marine life in this part of the Caribbean were really quite magnificent and unique. One afternoon, when we went snorkelling at one of the more secluded northern beaches, my companion handed me a spear gun as protection against overly inquisitive sharks and barracudas that frequented the area.

While there were many sharks and barracudas swimming around us, none showed any real interest in our presence. At one point, I dived down to a large rocky outcrop some 10 meters below the surface. When I looked into the murky water behind an overhang I had a brief glimpse of something large and colourful moving in the background, but I was unable to identify what it was. After returning to the surface to take a breath of fresh air, I went back down to the overhang where, hanging upside down holding on to a piece of rock with one hand, I pointed and fired the spear gun blindly into the space beyond the overhang.

When I retrieved the metal harpoon, which was attached to the gun by a nylon cord, I saw that I had speared a massive lobster through its carapace at the top of its thick tail. It was still very much alive and as it became exposed to the bright open water, it starting thrashing around with its huge tail with such force that it turned me in circles. I could do little to counteract its strength and continued to be turned in circles until I reached shallower water. When I finally stood up and lifted the lobster out of the water, it was that heavy that the harpoon bent so badly it couldn't be used again. The lobster, which a number of locals said was the biggest they had ever seen caught on the island, weighed in at over 30lbs, stood 3' tall from the tip of its claws to the bottom of the fan on its tail and with an 18" girth at the widest point of its tail. There wasn't a pot big enough on the island to cook it in one go. Ultimately, it fed ten men for two days after being boiled for 35 minutes on each side.

(B). LEGLESS CHRISTMAS

For most of my tour of duty on Anguilla, I was posted to a base camp known as 'Whisky Bravo', which was situated close to a commercial site full of salt pans. It consisted of a detached bungalow on the edge of a beautiful sandy beach surrounded by coconut trees. I became friendly with the local 'headsman', a fisherman of some renown, whom I regularly accompanied on night-fishing trips. He invited me to his home on Christmas Day morning for a celebratory drink, a prestigious honour for an outsider like myself. It would have been political suicide to decline such an offer or fail to turn up. However, I was also aware that islanders plied their guests with a locally brewed white rum known as 'mungy' (Mount Gay) rum. This 'fire water' was lethal and had an alcohol content off the scale. It should have come with a health-hazard warning, not to be drunk in the vicinity of smokers for fear of fire or explosion! Having been advised that this rum was potent and should only be consumed with a 'chaser', I played the diplomatic card by taking a 'six pack' of lager beer and two small thimble-sized glasses with me. During the short time I stayed with the 'headsman', I only drank two small glasses of rum and half a can of beer. When I returned to my quarters at 11.30am, I was pleased with myself as I felt fine and none the worse for wear.

At midday, the six constables, including myself, who resided at 'Whisky Bravo', were collected and transported to the main 'central' camp on the island where the army and police headquarters were located. On arrival, we went and joined the other police officers and Royal Engineers at the make-shift tented canteen, for our full roast Christmas Day lunch. We sat at long tables on wooden benches. I remember eating my main course, but thereafter I had no memory of anything that happened until I woke up on my bed at 'Whisky Bravo' at around 6.30pm. However, a colleague later told me that I polished off a second main meal before gracefully falling backwards off the bench onto the bare floor where I lay perfectly still, snoring for all I was worth. I was thrown into the rear of a truck and driven back to my billet, where I was dumped unceremoniously on my bed, completely oblivious of what had taken place; all thanks to two small glasses of 'mungy' rum. Therein lies a tale: don't imbibe when you don't know the consequences of you actions.

A friend woke me early evening on Christmas Day and asked me if I wished to join him and other colleagues at 'Papa Charlie', our police social club, for a party. Not wishing to be regarded as a miserable or unsociable party pooper, I joined the others, but because I felt so fragile I sat in a quiet, dimly lit corner of the club all evening, sipping straight tomato juices.

(C). WICKERS WORLD OF WONDER

During my tour of duty, the internationally famous broadcaster and reporter, Alan Wicker, arrived on the island to make a television programme about the events giving rise to the police occupation of Anguilla and what had occurred since then, to be incorporated in his travel series known as *Wickers World*. He travelled around the island filming and interviewing all and sundry. When he eventually arrived at my base at 'Whisky Bravo' with his small team of cameramen, like the prodigal son bearing gifts — two full crates of beer — we all spent some time introducing ourselves and getting involved in some pretty frivolous conversation. Throughout the time he was with us, approximately three hours, Alan was approachable, congenial and patient. I was impressed with his professionalism and courtesy, but I suppose I should not have expected less as, like all journalists, we had something he wanted and it was to his benefit to treat us with care and sensitivity.

Over the next few days, my initial impression of Alan Wicker took a bit of a nose dive, as my colleagues and I came into contact with him on several occasions but each time he gave us the 'cold shoulder' by ignoring us completely. In fact, on one occasion when I greeted him personally, he gave no verbal response, but simply looked at me as though I was some bug that had just crawled out from under a rock. Unfortunately for him, just prior to leaving Anguilla, he must have realised he had either missed something he needed to cover or required clarification on some point, because he approached several of us for a further interview. To a man, we politely declined his request for further assistance, which clearly annoyed him. His displeasure came in the form of a pretty direct and tardy verbal response, which gave no room for misunderstanding. It appeared that some of his attributes were only skin deep. Mr. Wicker was undoubtedly an intelligent and rather pompous individual, with a big ego, who was used to getting his own way. I suppose these features are only to be expected in someone who has reached his position. Nevertheless, while I was far from impressed with his negative features, I couldn't help but like the man and his silky smooth voice. The programme on Anguilla was broadcast on I.T.V. late in 1969, but I was a little disappointed, being so photogenic, that I only featured on screen for about 30 seconds!

ALBANY STREET DIVISION – 1972/1976

On being promoted to uniform sergeant in 1972, I was transferred to Albany Street Division ('ED'), within the Borough of Camden. It was an area suffering from social deprivation and decline, although there were a number of wealthy 'oases' dotted around its perimeter. The local community was made up predominantly of people of Irish 'labourer' extraction and emigrants from European countries with a Cypriot background. Busy commuter traffic traversed within its borders from three main railway termini; Kings Cross, St. Pancras and Euston Railway Stations.

While largely independent, with its own manpower and equipment resources, Tottenham Court Road Sub-Division ('ET') came under Albany Street's umbrella of responsibility and control with regard to administrative matters and senior management decisions on operational policing issues. Bearing in mind it was situated on the borders of the West End and Central London, its topography and affluence were significantly different to its neighbour. It contained a small residential community, many large businesses and a plethora of seedy bars and clubs. Although the volume of human traffic during the day was high, the area catered mainly for the evening and night-time leisure and entertainment industry for workers and visiting tourists. Sex-industry outlets, illegal gaming and alcohol establishments were in abundance.

I have very fond memories of my four and a half years on this division. It probably provided me with the greatest range and variety of practical day to day policing duties during my career, some examples of which are shown hereunder. It was undoubtedly one of the happiest times of my police service.

(A). COURTING ATTENTION

On the night in question, I had just taken over as the night duty charging sergeant at Albany Street Police Station. I was sitting at the charge room desk quietly minding my own business, checking the documentation for those prisoners already in custody, when two rowdy men in their twenties stomped into the room accompanied by a police constable who shepherded them to a secure bench at the back of the room. From their behaviour and speech it was clear that both men were the worse for wear from drinking alcohol; a fact the constable later confirmed when stating he had arrested them for being drunk and disorderly.

Although my concentration returned to the job at hand, I was aware that as the men sat on the bench they appeared to get more agitated. A few minutes later, as I got up from the desk to return the charge binder to its storage shelf, suddenly and without warning, both men rushed me. Before I knew what was happening and could take avoiding action, one of the men grabbed me around the neck from behind while the other grappled with me from the front trying to put me in a bear hug. Fortunately, the arresting officer quickly subdued the man on my back and returned him to the bench, giving me some clearance to deal with his companion. All of a sudden, the chap who was attempting to get a little too familiar with me, released his grip on my arms, stood back and took two wild swings with both fists which were directed towards my head. I managed to duck and swerve and only received a glancing blow to my right shoulder causing no discomfort. In response, I struck him once on the bridge of his nose with my left fist. He went limp and slumped to the floor. On hearing a crunch and seeing blood spurt from his nose, I assumed his nose was broken. While waiting for the divisional surgeon to arrive at the police station to administer treatment, both men were charged with the offence of being drunk and disorderly, the requisite documentation was completed and they were detained in police cells pending transfer to Old Street Magistrates' Court the next morning. In view of the fact they were drunk and no injury was sustained during their attack on me, I decided not to charge them with the additional offence of assault on police. This would have been viewed as excessive and a little like 'cracking a nut with a sledge hammer'.

When I arrived at court the following morning and saw the two men in the dock, they were clearly in a sorry state, particularly the fellow whose nose I had broken. He had a large bandage covering his nose and part of his face, with bruises showing around his eyes; he reminded me of a partially wrapped mummy! Both men pleaded guilty to the offence of drunk and disorderly and the arresting officer provided the court with the brief facts. However, instead of sitting down at this point, as was customary, and waiting for the magistrate's judgement, the man with the broken nose, who looked distinctly miserable and dejected, pointed at me and told the stipendiary magistrate that I had hit him and broken his nose. The magistrate immediately called me into the witness box and, under oath, asked me if the allegation was correct and what the surrounding circumstances were.

Upon completion of my evidence, the magistrate asked the prisoner if he agreed with my account. In reply the man said, "As God is my witness, your worship, I am innocent."

The magistrate considered his reply for a few seconds before saying, "He's not, I am, you're not, six months, and how dare you assault one of my officers."

Although given a six month prison sentence, in reality, he would probably have served a couple of weeks at most before release. However, had he kept his mouth shut about his broken nose, he would probably have received a 10 shilling (50 pence) fine and a dressing down, which is precisely the punishment his companion was given.

(B). PADDY POWER

As section sergeant on night duty, I had responsibility for ensuring all beat officers on the division were policing their designated beats appropriately. To aid me in this activity, I was driving a police 'panda' car, which gave me considerable flexibility in my movements and enabled me to respond to incidents requiring additional manpower without undue delay. On this particular mid-week night, which was usually pretty quiet, I had a young probationary constable with me for company. In truth, he was with me to learn; I relayed practical information of interest about the various beats as we passed through them and it gave him the opportunity to study the division's topography. While on mobile patrol at 10.45pm, an urgent assistance call came through on my 'personal radio' from the reserve (comms) officer at Albany Street Police Station. The message requested police attend the Oxford Arms public house, Camden High Street in the heart of Camden Town, where a disturbance was in progress. As the beat officer was the only person to accept the call, I advised the reserve officer that it was also my intention to lend my assistance.

On arriving and parking outside the front of the pub, we were met by a rather agitated and distressed licensee, who said that one of his regular customers, who had never before caused any problems, had suddenly lost the plot and gone on the rampage around the public bar, systematically damaging property. When I asked the licensee if the customer was drunk and whether anyone had received any physical injuries, he told me that although the customer had probably consumed at least 10 pints of Guinness that evening, he did not consider him to be drunk or even tipsy. He also told me that he was unaware of any injuries to his patrons, although he did add that during the mayhem most customers had managed to disburse and leave the pub. The licensee advised me to approach the perpetrator carefully, as he could be a 'handful'; well, that could have proved to be the understatement of the century! When asked where the man could be found, I was told he had retreated to the male toilets where he was calming down.

As I entered the premises I was confronted with a scene of utter carnage. The destruction and devastation of the public bar area was almost complete. Few items of furniture, fixtures or fittings remained intact; tables and chairs were overturned and smashed to pieces, bottles and glasses had been broken, with glass strewn all over the floor, and the dart board had been torn off the wall. Having observed the damage and spoken to a few of the remaining customers, my accompanying constable and I approached the gents' loos with caution and entered the urinal section where we came face to face with a 'man mountain'. He must have been six foot six inches tall if an inch, and almost as wide. His biceps were thicker than my thighs and the rest of his body was in proportion. I felt like an insignificant midget who was about to have sand kicked in his face and then be pummelled to a pulp. My first thoughts were that it was not my lucky day, and that there was a hospital bed out there somewhere with my name on it beckoning.

I could see that, while still a little agitated, he was under control and had all his faculties. When I enquired as to what had given rise to his violent outburst, he said it was a combination of a bad day at work, sad family news from Ireland and a highly emotional argument with his wife prior to going to the pub. Whilst he made no mention of it, I concluded that the amount of alcohol he had consumed had probably also been a contributory factor. He told me he was an Irish labourer known as Paddy to his friends; what a surprise! Shortly after I started talking to him, I realised he was contrite, apologetic and very co-operative. On being told that I would have to arrest him and convey him to the police station to be charged, he acknowledged he fully understood and accepted my course of action. To show that I had a handle on things (I don't think so) and was in full control of the situation (hope springs eternal), the constable and I took an arm each and led him out of the pub to a police van waiting by the kerb. When we reached the back of the van, he raised both arms in mock submission, lifting both of us off the ground with ease. It was at this time that I said a small prayer, which was pretty unusual and impressive for an agnostic, giving thanks for finding the only 'gentle giant' in a hard-nosed area like Camden.

(C). GAMBLING GALORE

Out of the four years I spent on Albany Street Division, almost half of my duty time was performed in plain clothes in charge of the local 'vice squad'. The type of work undertaken by this squad, which consisted of one experienced constable, henceforth referred to as my side-kick, and myself, not the biggest unit imaginable, included elements from the sex trade such as pornography, sauna and pimp work, the illegal sale of alcohol and illegal gaming. Apart from the Irish contingent, a large portion of the Camden residential community were emigrants with a Cypriot background from the Mediterranean. From research conducted on the Greek Cypriot community, it was established that they were partial to owning small private premises which they converted into cafés/social clubs, which were normally restricted to members from their own ethnic group. Furthermore, many from the male side of their community were compulsive or habitual gamblers. Put these factors together and it will come as no surprise to find that many of the clubs were used for gaming purposes as well as social discourse.

Before my 'bucko', sorry, side-kick, and I could even contemplate conducting surveillance operations on premises suspected of conducting illegal gaming, it was essential that we first learned how to play the relevant games and understood their rules. The most popular and frequent games played in these Cypriot cafes/social clubs were Kalooki (a derivative of the card game Rummy); Kunga, a European bastardisation of the card game Bastra; and Pokerisey (a form of poker). For the reader to comprehend the intricacies associated with a particular game and how it relates to the law, it would be helpful, but not essential, to get acquainted with the constituent parts of the game and how it is played. For a card game, or any other type of game, as a matter of fact, to be classified as illegal, it must 1) contain an element of 'chance' in it to win the game and 2) the 'house' (proprietor) who co-ordinates or permits his premises to be used for gaming, or the organiser running it, must either make a 'levy' charge on players (punters) authorising them to participate or take a 'cut' from a punter's winnings. It was the norm to charge a 'levy' of between 15–25%, whereas a 'cut' would normally be 5%. The reason for the disparity between the two charges was that the 'levy' was a single one-off charge, whereas a 'cut' was charged at the end of every game.

Surveillance was conducted in two ways, internally or externally. Obviously, the internal method was preferable, as it enabled both observation officers to be close to the seat of any possible offence, with one officer, usually myself, competing in the illegal gaming, while the other gathered evidence from a separate location nearby. While planning the approach to an operation and to assist officers who subsequently take part in a raid, it was imperative to ascertain accurate layouts of both the interior and exterior of the premises concerned. That's only the beginning, because to stand any realistic chance of obtaining a successful prosecution, it was also essential, in addition to presenting a detailed course of events during periods of observation, to establish and show the following:

1)   That the game was one of 'chance';
2)   The gaming was being controlled by the owner or proprietor of the premises or an independent 'organ-iser'/'croupier' working in conjunction with, or with the knowledge of, the owner;
3)   The denomination of the different coloured chips used in replacement of real money; actual cash was never used on the tables;
4)   Evidence showing that the owner/proprietor was charging punters a levy to play, how much they were being charged, when this was taken and, finally, where the money was stored;
5)   If it was a dedicated croupier who was taking a 'cut' from a winner's pot (winnings), proof of how and

when the cut was made (usually at the end of each game), how much was being charged (value of chips taken) and where 'cut' was stored (normally placed in a small basket set aside next to the croupier);

6) Detailed information relating to what gaming para- phernalia was being used. Failure to conduct proper research and background enquiries in connection with this type of operation, together with those factors highlighted above, will only ever happen once as the plain-clothes officers will draw the wrath of their divisional commander, be returned to normal foot duty forthwith and never be considered for plain- clothes duty again in the future while attached to the division. A lack of preparatory work, careful planning and execution **would** have catastrophic consequence on manpower and equipment resources, wastage of finance and inevitably lead to an embarrassing police failure and adverse publicity.

If my memory serves me well, my constable side-kick received reliable information from a source I was not privy to, it being accepted practice not to divulge the identity of informants, for understandable reasons, unless in an emergency. The information, which came to us early in February 1974, alleged that a Geek Cypriot club in Hampstead Road, NW1 some 100 yards north of Drummond Street, NW1, was regularly hosting illegal gaming. Before doing anything else, my side-kick and I did a comprehensive external survey on the premises and elicited the following data: it had a large solid wooden front door as entrance/exit, set at the back of an exceptionally wide pavement leading from a major highway; either side of the doorway were two big frosted widows cover- ing the entire frontage, with no view into the premises; both sides of the building were joined to other independent properties; the rear of the club was enclosed by flat-roofed garages behind a multistorey block of private flats which appeared accessible and, more importantly, the roof of the club was flat and laid with an asphalt membrane and a large glass skylight was situated in the middle giving a clear view into the centre of the premises. We also established that the club rarely opened before 5pm daily, apart from weekends when it tended to open at 2pm. I was satisfied with the results, as it meant we would probably be able to conduct a thorough external observation from the outside if we were unable to gain entry into the interior of the club. Accordingly, we then progressed onto the second phase of our recognisance, trying to secure entry.

Using various pretexts, we both managed to enter the premises twice on two separate occasions over the rest of February. Although neither of us gained the confidence or support of the proprietor, not being of Cypriot extraction, to remain on the premises for more than a few minutes, it did give us an ideal opportunity to record its layout, identify the owner and other employees and remember who they were for future reference. We were also able to confirm that there was no rear exit to the club, which also functioned as a café serving light refreshments; that there was a serving bar and till on one side of the main room, which also contained eight tables, four of which were purpose built 'baize' card tables and a large glass skylight in the centre of the ceiling, which was wide open every time we visited, no doubt to clear the smokey atmosphere and get some fresh air circulating throughout the club. While we were unwelcome to stay and use the club facilities, I was extremely pleased with the outcome of our internal reconnaissance, which clearly indicated gaming was taking place inside the premises. Our next task was to prepare our method of approach and conduct the surveillance operation. It should be born in mind that this type of work was very time-consuming as, albeit not imperative, it was force policy to conduct three separate periods of surveillance in every case of suspected illegal gaming. Being conscious of the weather conditions at that time of year, coupled with the fact of not wishing to draw undue attention to ourselves while we gained access to the club's roof via the rear garages etc, and being careful not to make any perceptible noise on the roof which could be detectable to patrons inside the club, I realised that this particular operation would probably involve long, strenuous, cold, wet and tedious periods of duty, with little time for refreshment, other than what we were able to take with us and even less time for relief purposes. Not exactly an appealing prospect!

When the day eventually arrived for our first observation, we were pumped up with enthusiasm and adrenalin and couldn't wait to get started, as everything had been planned so meticulously. You wouldn't believe just how crestfallen and frustrated I felt when the first thing I saw sitting at a table directly beneath the skylight was one of the senior uniform sergeants I knew from my police station, sitting at a table in civilian clothing, talking and playing cards with other customers. This was a potentially disastrous situation, as it certainly interrupted and prolonged our work on this case and could have even resulted in the job being completely compromised. In the circumstances, after consulting my side-kick, who was in agreement, I made an executive decision to nip the problem in the bud by immediately calling off our observation for that day. By doing so, there was no proof, just supposition, that the sergeant was engaged in illegal gaming. Although offences associated with illegal gaming are restricted to those owning, controlling and charging people to play, it may well have been construed by the powers to be, that had the sergeant been playing in an illegal game, that it was tantamount to aiding and abetting a criminal offence; not something to be recommended as it would have placed him in an invidious position.

This was without doubt the first pivotal time in my career and one I felt distinctly uncomfortable with. In the prevailing circumstances, I decided to take no further action and let the matter sink into oblivion. I knew that my correct course of action was to report the situation to my superiors and let the matter take its course. However, I was conscious that to do so could have led to severe, unpleasant and possibly career-changing consequences for the sergeant concerned, who was coming to the end of his career. With the potentially harsh repercussions, based on such flimsy information, a decision to report the matter weighed heavily on my shoulders. Although my decision was clinically wrong, at least I would be able to sleep easy at night! I have to admit that in addition to the above, I also tried to justify my actions by saying to myself that even if the sergeant had been playing in an illegal game, he wasn't committing an offence himself and that his involvement was of a minor nature. Probably, I'm simply trying to mitigate my own complicity in the case; I will let you decide! Without doubt, there will be those 'police bashers', sceptics and cynics out there in the public domain who will rush at the chance to castigate me for the decision I made, well, all I can say is they would have to live with their consciences. I find it hard to believe that faced with a similar situation themselves, they would not act in a similar manner, unless of course they were totally devoid of any human emotion, consciences or were missing their half 'brain cell'!

In view of the circumstances, coupled with my annoyance and frustration, I took it upon myself to confront the sergeant concerned while he was on duty one day soon after seeing him in the club. I told him what I had seen, my decision in respect of the situation, and strictly warned him not to return to the premises again under any circumstances and that if I had the slightest suspicion that the conduct of the club, its owners or the gaming conducted therein had changed in any way, I would have no hesitation in reporting him immediately for disciplinary proceedings to be considered. I hasten to add, I never had any reason to believe he visited the club again and the conduct of the premises did not change one iota from the time of our first observation.

Eventually, we successfully concluded our surveillance operation and acquired more than enough evidence to present before a court. The raiding party, consisting of a uniform inspector, one sergeant and twelve constables, were briefed by myself prior to the raid taking place. When the raid was underway, my side-kick and I were on the roof of the club directing the police staff to the appropriate places and people. The owner and his croupier were reported for the offence of illegal gaming, to be subsequently summoned to appear before the court and all property remotely connected with the gaming, including the tables, cards and chips were seized and placed in police storage. A successful prosecution ensued and the court issued a destruction order for all the gaming paraphernalia that was seized; this was subsequently disposed of in accordance with the court's instructions.

You may well ask why I decided to exhibit this particular case as one of my examples, especially since it was one of many I completed during my time on Albany Street Division, particularly when there were no doubt others of greater complexity and scale. The answer is simple: I have greater clarity and focus about this case, probably due to the rather unusual and awkward circumstances surrounding it.

(D). PROSTITUTION OR IMPORTUNING, THAT IS THE QUESTION

Minding our own business with time on our hands between jobs, my police constable assistant, better known as my side-kick, and I, decided to visit the Kings Cross Railway Station area one pleasant evening in late March 1974, with a view to seeing if any known 'pimps' were hanging around, working any of their girls in the oldest trade in the world, that of prostitution. At approximately 8pm, while standing amongst a small crowd outside the main exit/entrance to the station, we suddenly saw what appeared to be an attractive young woman, or so we thought, walking up and down the opposite pavement next to St. Pancras Railway Station. As men of the world using our combined knowledge of the opposite sex, which subsequently proved to be inadequate, we assumed from her actions and furtive movements, she was plying her wares for prostitution.

We split up and crossed the road to join the young woman on the same pavement she was on, but from opposite directions. Although our approach was stealthy, relaxed and unassuming, the woman, henceforth known as our 'target', was concentrating so much on what she was doing that she wasn't ever aware of our presence. She approached the kerb, where a car was stationary, and bent down by the passenger's window and appeared to have a brief conversation with the male driver before standing up again and walking away in my direction. At the time, I was leaning against a wall near the junction with Euston Road and I watched as two more 'punters' in their cars 'kerb crawled' down Pancras Road towards our 'target'. The first vehicle drove past her, but then drew up against the kerb next to another female prostitute plying her trade. However, the second vehicle stopped next to my target, who once again appeared to have a brief conversation with the male driver through the front passenger's window, before the door opened and she got into the nearside front seat. The car then drove off down Pancras Road away from me and out of sight. My side-kick and I joined forces again and decided to stay within the area, as most prostitutes working in it had a tendency to return to the same spot from where they were picked up to continue working, as there was usually a good supply of 'punters'.

It would be helpful, at this stage, if the reader understood what the definition of prostitution means and what constitutes an offence of prostitution legally. Basically, prostitution is an act where a female plies her body and/or offers sexual services for gain (money); the amount is irrelevant. In order to guarantee a good chance of achieving a prosecution for prostitution, it will be necessary to prove that:

1)   The woman was overtly plying her body for, or offering to engage in, sexual services.

2)   She was providing those services for gain, e.g. selling them for money.

3) That they must have received at least two official cautions for prostitution, kept in the central register/index held by police at New Scotland Yard (N.S.Y.), before they can be arrested and charged for the first time with an offence of prostitution.

4) Once arrested, a woman no longer needs to be cautioned before she can be arrested again.

5) Prior to arrest, a prostitute needs to be seen plying her wares on at least two separate occasions during a single period of observation, which can be either close together or several hours apart.

6) While not essential, it is always helpful to try and establish the level of charges made by the prostitute for the different service she offers; masturbation usually attracts a £10 charge, a 'blow job' (oral sex) normally costs £15 and full intercourse generally costs between £20–£25. This sort of information was not usually acquired until a suspect was questioned prior to arrest following caution or subsequent to arrest before charge. Other useful evidence that can often be gained relates to the property found on her person when searched after arrest at the police station, in the form of contraceptives and how many are in her possession.

If a female fulfils the criteria of overtly approaching different men for the purposes of having sex for cash, whether witnessed or suspected, she may justifiably be stopped and confronted with what has been seen and questioned. If the officer dealing with a potential prostitute is satisfied that she was committing an offence, he would first ask her for her personal details and conduct a check with N.S.Y. to confirm whether she is who she says she is and is already the subject of two formal cautions and can be arrested or she simply needs to be given at least one further caution and then be released. Most prostitutes who have been on the 'game' for some time will be well aware of these requirements and regularly use several different aliases, which result in them getting numerous official cautions before finally being arrested for the first time.

Our 'target' returned to Pancras Road within half an hour and no sooner had she been dropped off by the driver of the car, she started looking for further punters. However, before we were able to approach her, a different vehicle pulled up next to the kerb where she was standing. As before, she approached the front passenger's window, had a brief conversation with the male driver and got into the vehicle, which then drove away. We stayed close by the pick-up point in the hope that she would return to it. Fortunately for us, she returned within 20 minutes to the exact spot, which allowed me to approach the driver before he could drive away from the scene and enabled my side-kick to, simultaneously, confront our 'target'. When I first started questioning the driver of the car, he was adamant that she was his girlfriend. However, when I explained what we had observed during the evening and offered him the opportunity of attending court to speak as a witness on her behalf, his confidence evaporated and he began to retract what he had said earlier. After confirming his identity from documentation, his sole concern was that we did not contact him at his home address as this would cause his wife to become suspicious! Allowing him to drive off, I then joined my side-kick and our 'target'. Standing close to her for the first time, I could tell that our initial assessment of her was correct; she was attractive, looked to be in her late twenties, had a good figure, was about 5' 7" tall and spoke well with a refined medium-pitched voice.

While I had been dealing with the car diver, my side-kick had checked her details against those held at New Scotland Yard and had come back with a positive result. We were informed that our young lady was well known to police, having had three official cautions already recorded against the name she had provided. As further confirmation, her description also matched that contained on her register entry at N.S.Y. As a consequence, I cautioned and arrested her and then conveyed her to Albany Street Police Station where she was charged with the offence of 'soliciting for the purpose of prostitution'. Although I believed we had finally obtained her correct personal details, she was nevertheless detained in custody overnight in a female cell for direct transfer to court the following morning, as her particulars could not be confirmed.

After an early morning check by a woman police constable (W.P.C.), who gave my female prisoner some breakfast, the officer came to find me and suggested I return with her to the cell, as there was something strange about the prostitute. I accompanied the W.P.C. back to the cell where, at close quarters, I saw that there was a distinct growth of stubble pushing through my prisoner's facial make-up and that her breasts appeared to have reduced in size. I suddenly realised that I was probably dealing with a man, but because of some of the female characteristics attributed to her earlier, I decided that further confirmation would be prudent. Accordingly, I instructed the woman constable to conduct a physical body search, while I remained outside the cell close at hand should assistance be required. After a couple of minutes a small squeal emanated from the cell and I was summoned. On entering the cell I noticed that my prisoner's skirt had been removed and that she was wearing a pair of female knickers. It was now that she became a positive he, as his penis and testicles were strapped up towards his belly button with several strips of surgical sticky tape. I hurriedly notified the early turn charging sergeant of my discovery and the charge was altered to one of 'importuning', the male equivalent. On attending court later that morning, he pleaded guilty, was fined and then released to return home.

While we found the entire incident a little embarrassing and a bit of a knock to our male egos having been fooled into believing he was a woman, there was some solace to be taken in the fact that he had duped other police officers on at least three previous occasions in the West End of London. I console myself by saying that he was a much more attractive and realistic woman than he was a man!

(E). CASSETTE PORNOGRAPHY

Offences of a pornographic nature are, in general, not as complex, intense or time consuming as many others requiring some element of surveillance work. Furthermore, similar to gaming offences, pornography does not constitute an arrestable offence. Offenders are cautioned and reported at the scene of the alleged crime, with a view to being summoned before a court subsequently. The level of evidence required to procure a satisfactory conviction is also relatively uncomplicated in comparison to many other offences within the sex trade.

Once there is reasonable suspicion that pornographic material was being sold on certain premises, the officer in possession of the requisite information would need to attend the local magistrates' court in order to swear out a warrant 'in camera' (private), before a magistrate, to search those premises. This type of search warrant normally has to be executed within a period of one month. At the earliest opportunity after suspected material has been confiscated, it must be checked thoroughly and individually to confirm whether or not it contains pornography. Any items found not to be pornographic would immediately be returned to the owner. In the eyes of the law, material would only be classified as pornographic if it contained any view of a sexual act in progress, down to a simple display of an erect male penis or 'open view' of female genitalia.

In September 1974 I received information from a number of different sources, indicating that pornographic literature was being sold from premises situated in Evershalt Street at the junction with Grafton Place, NW1. Around this time, there had been a steady growth in the number of shops selling material of a sexual nature in and around the area of the West End of London. It was felt that this increased popularity in this type of business was due, in the main, to the transition from '8 millimetre reels' of porn film to DVD cassettes used in modern television recorders. DVD production tended to be of better quality, less bulky, easier to transport and secrete and could be used in conjunction with a T.V. set without the need for a separate projector.

Initial recognisance revealed that the property we were interested in had only recently been opened and had been adapted for the sale of books and magazines. However, when my side-kick (an experienced police constable) and I entered the premises independently on a number of different occasions purporting to be ordinary customers, neither of us saw any pornographic material on show. Although all the items of literature on display e.g. books, magazines and leaflets were predominantly of a sexual nature, the contents were, however, no more than legal soft porn. Further enquiries revealed that the pornographic literature was apparently being kept out of sight behind and below the shop counter and only sold to 'regular' customers who had gained the confidence and trust of the shop keeper. Owing to the relatively small size of the shop counter, we felt it was highly unlikely that the proprietor would maintain a large stock. Over the next few weeks my side-kick managed to establish and develop a good rapport and relationship with the shop owner, who eventually stated he would be able to sell him 'hard core' porn whenever he wanted it. He also indicated that he possessed a good variety of porn by briefly showing him a box from beneath the counter purporting to contain such items.

Within a couple of days I managed to obtain the necessary authority and funds from my divisional commander to make a 'test purchase'. My side-kick made the 'test purchase', after carefully and quite deliberately looking through the stock he was presented with from beneath the counter. His DVD cassette selection was just one of those he considered was probably 'hard core' porn. I was present in the shop at the time the purchase was made and was in such close proximity that I saw everything that took place. As soon as we returned to the police station we viewed the cassette and confirmed that it consisted of material which was exclusively of an illegal pornographic nature. A search warrant was obtained and within a few days a small raiding party was put together, consisting of one uniform sergeant and five constables under the leadership of an inspector. When the raid was eventually undertaken, neither my side-kick or I were involved in it, as it was desirable that we retained our anonymity for future use. However, we remained in the vicinity to render advice and give assistance had it been required. When we returned to Albany Street Police Station upon completion of the raid to catalogue and provide a comprehensive list of the seized items, I was quite surprised over the volume of suspected pornographic material that had been confiscated from such a small shop. Apart from about 50 magazines, there were in excess of a hundred DVDs and 8mm reels of film of a suspicious nature. I must admit that the thought of having to view all the items individually, albeit only to the point when 'hard core' porn was identified, did appear to be a rather daunting prospect.

I set aside an entire 'late turn' tour of duty (2pm–10pm) to complete, or at least break the back of, the checking and confirmation process to determine the pornographic content of the items seized. I instructed my side-kick to make all peripheral and equipment arrangements to facilitate and expedite our task. Unbeknown to me at the time, my side-kick bumped into our divisional commander who, in his wisdom, after being told of the outcome of the raid and what we were intending to do that day, decided he wanted to participate in the viewing process. I'd like to think his interest was purely professional and he was not just being a 'dirty old man', the chance would be a fine thing, but I don't think I could convince anyone that that was truly the case! You can imagine my surprise when I reported for duty to be told by my assistant that the chief superintendent's office had been set aside for us to use to view the material, to prevent us being interrupted or disturbed. My consternation increased significantly when I arrived in his office to find several chairs lined up in rows occupied by many of the senior staff at the police station, together with a few stragglers, waiting for 'the show to begin'. Even more infuriating was the fact that my deputy and I were expected to act as commentator and projectionist. Instead of viewing only a small portion of each item, I was pressurised by those above me to show some items to the end, thereby prolonging the job at hand; it took another full day before we completed the task.

By the time we had completed the task of viewing all the material, of which only a few items were not 'hard core', I have to admit that I was sick to my stomach. Although, initially, the novelty spiked my interest, particularly in connection with stories involving normal sexual activity between men and women, it didn't take long before I got bored and tired with that. However, there were also real examples of bestiality, homosexuality, lesbianism, child porn, and various other gruesome sexual deviations we had to view. While no one could accuse me of being a prude, I have to say that I found most of the material inhuman, demeaning, belittling, pathetic and just down right disgusting; for a short time, I actually felt ashamed to a member of the human race. When I got home that night and told my wife what I had been doing at work all that day, I remember her saying, with some measure of concern in her voice, "Well, I hope you haven't brought any funny ideas home." My reply was something to the effect that the only funny idea I had was that I had absolutely no interest in sex at that time.

To be completely honest, I find it incomprehensible how anyone could derive any degree of pleasure or satisfaction from such depraved material. People who do, and I know they exist, are, in my considered opinion, sick in mind and in desperate need of serious psychological help.

(F). CARE AND CONSIDERATION

Relations between the police and social services were often tenuous at best during much of my police career, particularly in those poorer socialist areas in and around London. Social workers were seen by many police officers as slightly left wing, scruffy pseudo intellectuals, with plenty of theoretical knowledge and good intentions, but completely bereft of practical ability and common sense. Police officers, on the other hand, were viewed by their counterparts in the social services as those hard, inflexible representatives of authority who failed to exhibit emotion at appropriate times.

On a particularly cold and bitter Saturday night in November 1974, at about 12.30am while performing the duty of uniform section sergeant, I received a message from an anonymous caller requesting my attendance at a large block of council flats, where it was alleged young children had been abandoned. As precise details of the flat were supplied, both the local beat officer and myself accepted the call and cautiously made our way to the third floor landing of the building where the flat was located. The first thing I noticed upon my arrival was that there was no landing light outside the premises. The reason for this was clearly apparent, as a piece of electrical wiring had been connected to the socket points where the light bulb should have been. This piece of wiring then entered the flat via a gap in the top of the kitchen window. The front door of the flat was ajar and a large pane of glass next to it, which was part of a bedroom window, had been smashed, leaving the flat open to the elements.

When the beat constable had joined me, we entered the flat through the open front door and walked down the hallway trying the light switches, but there was clearly no electrical supply to the property. The atmosphere inside of the flat was extremely cold, musty and damp and there was a strong smell of urine permeating throughout the premises. Having no source of electricity, we were forced to use our torches and the first thing I saw when I switched mine on, was a load of animal excrement lying on the hallway carpet in a number of different places. Animal faeces was also present on the lounge floor, together with a large quantity of other rubbish. I then entered the kitchen to be confronted with the disgusting sight of a double sink full of filthy cutlery and crockery. There was green mould covering most of the cups and plates and various different types of knives were lying about on the work surfaces.

While studying the situation in the kitchen, the Beat constable summoned me to a bedroom, where he had found two young children, a girl aged seven and a boy aged four, in a semiconscious state. Although there were two single beds in the room, the children were found hugging each other in one of the beds which was sodden by their urine. The children, who were only wearing thin nightwear, were shivering with cold, which was hardly surprising since there was only a lightweight sheet and one blanket on the bed. Lying on the floor beside the bed was a large kitchen knife, which I narrowly missed stepping on. I left these children with the beat constable, pending the arrival of a female police officer, whose attendance I had requested, to provide practical assistance and emotional support. I then went to the last room in the flat, a second small bedroom, where I found a full sized child's pram. Looking inside the pram, I was rather surprised to find a small baby, which turned out to be a six-month-old boy, lying on a mattress of urine and poop. Since the excrement was about an inch thick in the bottom of the pram and the smell emanating from it was almost unbearable, it was apparent that the situation had been of long standing. As the baby looked to be in poor physical condition and there was little response from him, I called for an ambulance to convey him to hospital for treatment.

We spent about an hour at the flat, during which time we neither saw nor were we approached by any adult. As a consequence, I made some local enquiries with neighbours and established that the children lived in the flat with their mother; there had never been any sign of a father. Information also came to hand indicating that the mother was an unemployed alcoholic who regularly solicited for prostitution in the Kings Cross area. In view of the circumstances, I took both older children into 'safe' police custody and conveyed them to Albany Street Police Station, where I initiated a 28-day 'interim' care order before handing the children over into the care of the social services. It was subsequently disclosed that when the six- month-old boy was initially admitted to hospital, he was suffering from pneumonia.

Within two weeks of the original incident and the children being placed into temporary care, the head of social services organised a meeting to be held at their headquarters in Camden Town, to discuss what future action was considered prudent in connection with the family. During the meeting, which involved representatives from all the agencies who had been in contact with the family, a very senior member from the social services suggested that, as a form of appeasement to the mother for taking her children away from her, the six-month-old infant should be returned to her custody to live at home. He had by then recovered from pneumonia and regained his health. This proposal was clearly intended as some sort of interim measure to keep the mother content pending a decision being made as to the final action to be taken with regard to the children. Because of this proposal, I assumed that the social services were not particularly supportive of applying for a 'full' care order.

I found it absolutely incredulous that, bearing in mind the background circumstances of this case, that someone in such a high position of authority would ever contemplate returning the infant back into the custody of its mother. Such a proposal was professionally inept and completely lacking in common sense. To show my displeasure and annoyance, I addressed the 'chair' of the meeting and requested that the minutes of the meeting record that I strongly objected to the proposal, and that should it be approved it would probably end up with a similar result as occurred in the Maria Colwell case; an incident involving the murder of a young girl, where social services involvement attracted serious criticism. Following my outburst, the proposal was dropped immediately and it was agreed, unanimously, that the only justifiable further course of action was to apply for a 'full' care order. Responsibility for the future care and attention of the three children then passed to the social services until they reached the legal age of adulthood and independence.

(G). A SENTIMENTAL OCCASION

While not of any real significance in the bigger picture, the following example is one of the few that, even now, leaves me with a warm feeling and a sense of achievement. I find it quite amazing, yet pleasing, that it is often the smaller things in life that give us the greatest pleasure and satisfaction; this case certainly falls within that category. Without doubt, this was a rather rare and unique incident, with an unusual set of circumstances. It would be fair to say that my handling of it was also somewhat strange and unorthodox and would have raised the eyebrows of many of my supervisors. Irrespective of the fact that there was nothing intrinsically wrong with my approach, it did contain a level of emotion and sentimentality not normally attributed to police work. Normally, my reaction would have been more clinical and constrained in line with the basic legal requirements and police training.

One Friday evening in early June 1975, I was at a bit of a loose end working alone, my constable side-kick being away for a few days on annual leave, when I decided to visit the Kings Cross area to see if there was anything of interest going on worthy of later attention. At about 8pm, while ambling along the concourse at Kings Cross Railway Station, my attention was drawn to an attractive young woman who nearly collided with me while searching through her handbag. I was, and still am, unable to determine the reason for my subsequent actions, save to say that they were probably due to a sixth sense or gut feeling. For no apparent reason I was riveted to the spot concentrating on her every movement. She seemed to be unsure of herself, indecisive as to what she wanted to do next and oblivious to everything going on around her. On a number of occasions she stopped dead in her tracks, deep in thought for a couple of minutes before moving off again. All of a sudden it appeared that she had finally made a decision, as she purposely strode off towards Pancras Road. She eventually stopped near the junction with Euston Road where, amongst a lot of moving human traffic, which she totally ignored, she watched the antics of a couple of local prostitutes plying their trade further down Pancras Road. For about half an hour she continued to observe the prostitutes, ignoring everything else going on around her, when suddenly and incredulously, she walked slowly and purposely up to the front nearside door of a 'kerb-crawler' that had pulled up beside her. She stooped down, had a brief conversation with the driver, got into the front passenger's seat and then drove off.

As most prostitutes who worked this area came back to the spot where they were picked up to continue working, I remained in the vicinity in the hope of accosting her should she return. Within 20 minutes I saw her dropped off a little further down Pancras Road and the car drive off. I walked towards her, but before I reached her position she had already started to talk to the driver of a new 'kerb-crawling' vehicle. Unaware of my approach, she was, understandably, a little alarmed and apprehensive when I pulled her to one side and started speaking to her. In an effort to dispel her concerns, I immediately introduced myself and told her what I had observed. After obtaining her personal details, which were confirmed against documents in her possession, a most unusual occurrence when dealing with prostitutes, I conducted a check with the central index at N.S.Y. where it was confirmed that no one by her name had previously received an official caution for prostitution. Accordingly, I informed her that, while she would not be arrested, she would be in receipt of a formal caution.

I quickly realised I was dealing with a completely different type of female to the ones who normally solicited for prostitution on the streets around Kings Cross. In comparison to those prostitutes, who were normally hard-nosed, abrasive, argumentative, defensive, uncooperative and from a working class background, my young woman, for that was what she was, having confirmed she was only 17 years of age, was polite, intelligent, cooperative, sensitive, articulate, well spoken, and pleasantly mannered. It was obvious to me that she was naïve, very inexperienced, lacking in common sense and maturity but, more importantly, she was placing herself in a position of potential serious danger. Instead of letting her depart and go her own way after cautioning her, which would have been correct course of action, I pressurised her to accept an invitation to accompany me to a local café to have a relaxing chat over a cup of coffee. Albeit somewhat tense in the beginning, it didn't take long before we both relaxed and conversation flowed easily. I established that she was an intelligent young woman, who was at that time attending college studying for her 'A' levels, that she lived with her parents and a brother in a privately owned detached house in Nottingham, that she came from a close loving family who were financially independent and lived a comfortable life wanting for nothing. She told me that she knew a girl at her school who had solicited around the Kings Cross area who told her how easy it was to make a good amount of money offering sexual favours. She also stated, quite categorically, that she would only engage in acts of 'male' masturbation. In response, I informed her of the dangers associated with multiple sexual activities in connection with contracting various sexual diseases. I also warned her of the strong possibility that she would attract the attention of a 'pimp', who would put her in fear, control her working life, take her money and probably treat her in a cruel and violent manner. I made it patently clear that it was not recommended for her to continue to pursue her current path and that I did not expect to see her again. Apart from giving her a lot to think about on her way home, I got the impression that I had also got through to her.

While engaged on another task the following Friday evening, I was flabbergasted when, at about 9.30pm as I passed along Pancras Road, I saw the young woman I had dealt with the previous week being dropped off by a 'punter'. Although not in possession of any substantive evidence against her, which would justify either arrest or caution, I knew she would be unaware of that fact. Driven by anger, frustration and a sense of responsibility for her welfare, I immediately intercepted her on the pretext of having witnessed her actions. While I knew I was skating on thin ice, I not only kept up my pretence but even exaggerated it a little, by dramatising the potential legal consequences of her behaviour. Having already used the rational approach, with little or no noticeable success, I considered it was then time to employ more frightening and draconian tactics.

After getting over the initial shock of seeing me again and listening to the disappointment in my voice, she appeared genuinely crestfallen and apologetic. I took advantage of her contrite mood by making her an offer which, had she declined, would not have received the slightest consideration let alone implementation. The proposal was simple but direct, I told her that I would not caution or arrest her on this occasion, but if I ever saw her again or even heard a whisper that she was still soliciting for prostitution, I would have no hesitation in arresting her and throwing the full force of the law at her, in addition to notifying her parents of the full circumstances leading to her apprehension. I knew that the latter threat was probably the strongest leverage I could apply, as she had strong family ties.

I never did see her again, although a couple of months later I received a letter from her, addressed to Albany Street Police Station, thanking me for my assistance and assuring me that she had got her life back on track. About a year later, I checked with the central index of prostitute cautions and discovered that, with the exception of the caution I had administered in June 1975, she had not come to notice again. I was satisfied that, with a little bit of help from yours truly, she had avoided taking a downward slippery slope in her life. To help just one person in such a positive way, made me feel good about myself and the job I was doing.

NOTTING HILL CARNIVAL – August 1976

On the 30th August 1976, I was on a short foot patrol, together with other members from my serial (1 inspector, 2 sergeants, 20 constables) and numerous other officers, policing the Notting Hill Carnival, a festival celebrating the Caribbean culture along the streets in West London. With numerous colourful parades, floats and steel bands traversing the area, the atmosphere was, initially, very relaxed, convivial and friendly. On the whole, those police officers in attendance mixed harmoniously with the multi-racial crowd, as everyone enjoyed the festivities. The area was a seething mass of humanity in perpetual motion. While the crowd consisted of many different nationalities, young Afro-Caribbeans predominated.

As the afternoon progressed, there was a palpable change in the mood of the black youths frequenting the carnival. Tensions were rising as incidents of street crime increased with a commensurate police response. Groups of youths, both black and white, began wandering around the Portabello Road and Ladbrook Grove areas apparently looking for trouble. Reports of street robberies, pick-pocket thefts, drug-taking incidents and assaults against revellers, became more frequent as darkness enveloped the area. The catalyst for the first act of violence against the police occurred when a young black pick-pocket was arrested. A group of young black youths in the vicinity took umbrage at this action and started jostling and assaulting the officers. In next to no time, all hell seemed to break loose as police officers started to engage in running street battles.

While the police were the butt of the early violence, as the disorder intensified it became more indiscriminate. Shops, vehicles and private residence soon became the subject of attack and it didn't take long before the surrounding area looked like a bomb site. As the violence increased so did the selection of weapons; bricks, concrete, bottles, wood batons, stones and various metal objects were hurled at the police, who in turn grabbed any object within easy reach to protect themselves. Those of us who were deployed early in the day, were dressed in our normal uniforms without any protective equipment. As a consequence, we were open to attack and injury without recourse to retaliation. Items within police disposal included dustbin lids, empty milk crates and pieces of cardboard. I managed to grab a metal dustbin lid, which must have looked hilarious to any bystander. However, as ludicrous as it may have appeared, it saved me from serious injury on a number of occasions.

At one point a large crowd drove my small contingent of constables down a cul-de-sac with no visible exit point. As we sustained a continuous barrage of missiles and I saw some of my personnel getting injured, I began to think we were all going to end up in hospital, at best. Suddenly, we were released from our predicament by a serial of police officers who disbursed the crowd from their rear. Fortunately, although some of my constables and I required minor medical treatment for abrasions, no serious injuries were sustained.

The majority of the public who attended the carnival, irrespective of ethnicity, were law abiding people who, as so often is the case, became embroiled in the situation because of their proximity to it. I can say without fear of contradiction, that anyone visiting the festival during the afternoon and evening on that fateful day, would have found the experience both frightening and daunting. By late evening, when the majority of people had departed from the area and police action had subsided, the disorder eventually petered out. As we were being dismissed to return to our respective divisions licking our wounds, I became aware that the toll of police injuries and arrests were high, which didn't surprise me in the least, as the violence towards the police was intense and prolonged.

When the dust had settled, I was astonished and once again annoyed, to find that certain sections of the media, better known as the 'gutter press', had criticised police involvement in the Notting Hill Carnival. They suggested the police were responsible for the riot by applying 'arbitrary harassment'. It never ceases to amaze me how bigoted some people can be, where common decency and the truth are overshadowed by political dogma and misguided beliefs. Apart from denying the above accusation, I would pose the following question: 'Are the Police, who are employed to uphold law and order, expected to simply sit back and do nothing when criminal offences are committed in front of them by minority groups, for fear of a hostile response?' The answer has got to be NO if anarchy in society is to be avoided.

PICKLED BEETROOT OR WALNUTS, WHAT A BUMMER – 1977/1978

In 1977 I was seconded to the Criminal Investigation Bureau (CIB2) at New Scotland Yard, as a temporary detective sergeant and member of a small select team investigating the re-cycling of a large quantity of drugs from police custody back into the public domain. Although this branch would not feature on my favourites list, it was known for being beneficial from a career perspective. The bureau had responsibility for the investigation of 'internal' police complaints, of both a disciplinary and criminal nature.

On my arrival, I was attached to a detective chief superintendent (DCS) and we worked together as a team within a team. In reality, my role was little more than 'gofer'/'bag carrier'. While my supervisor (DCS) did nothing to upset me during our time together, I fail to understand, even to this day, how he ever managed to reach such a high rank, as I never encountered a more inept senior officer during my entire career. In this particular case, the saying 'people are often promoted to their level of incompetency' was clearly an understatement. He was very conscious of his humble origins and did everything in his power to try and convince others that he came from higher, more prestigious stock.

My DCS had the reputation for being a pompous, arrogant and self-opinionated individual. I wouldn't disagree with that assessment, other than to say he was also a supercilious prat. He was the only officer I knew who took his privately owned desk everywhere he went, irrespective of the fact that the Service provided good quality furniture free of charge. Admittedly, it was a beautiful piece of solid polished mahogany, but far too large for the average office. Apart from fulfilling my own tasks, I often had to complete many of his duties or remind him to do certain things which should have been done automatically by him. Whether this arose out of basic laziness on his part or lack of ability I will never know. While my time working with him was far from memorable or enjoyable, there were two specific incidents which, even now, still bring a wry smile to my face.

On the morning after our bureau's Christmas party, I was rather bruskly and unceremoniously ordered to present myself before my DCS in his office. I was confronted by a disconsolate and miserable-looking boss, who disdainfully pointed to the top of his desk. There, beautifully preserved on the glistening desk top surface was the outline of two perfectly shaped female buttocks, which were accompanied by some pubic hair lying close by. Although I had a good idea who the amorous lovers were, I played 'possum' and offered no incentive to my boss to instigate any further action. Realising he wasn't getting anywhere, he directed me to clean and polish his desk top. In for a bit of dig, yes, but well worth the pleasure it gave me.

On another occasion, when we were staying at a hotel pending completion of enquiries some distance away from our base, we met for dinner in the hotel's up-market restaurant. Prior to placing our respective orders the DCS pointed to a brown mass on a plate on an adjoining table and stated how much he enjoyed pickled beetroot. I assume he was trying to impress me, but I looked at him somewhat quizzically as I couldn't see the beetroot he was referring to. His order was a little more elaborate than mine, as his expense allowance was more generous. Shortly after we started eating he suddenly spat something out onto his side plate and exclaimed, "These beetroots are off." As he tried to get the attention of the waiter, I noticed that what he was referring to was the same brown mass he had earlier pointed to on the plate at the adjoining table, which was, in reality, pickled **walnuts.** When the waiter eventually arrived at our table and explained the situation, the DCS looked distinctly sheepish and a little embarrassed. I must admit I had a good laugh at his expense. This was yet another glaring example of him showing he was not as conversant with the finer points in life as he would have wished to be.

ROMFORD DIVISION 1979/1981 – DRIVING DISASTERS

Shortly after my promotion to the rank of uniform Inspector, I was transferred to Romford Division, one of the largest policing areas in the eastern sector of the M.P.S. It incorporated the sub-divisions of Romford, Hornchurch, Rainham and Upminster. Being largely an urban residential area interspersed with businesses in and around the local towns, it also contained three major arterial highways, the A12, A13 and A127, traversing throughout its length and breadth.

During the two and a half years I spent on the division, I performed shift work with 'relief' officers in addition to taking on the mantle of unit commander at both Hornchurch and Upminster Police Stations. As there was never a dull moment at work, boredom and stagnation rarely arose. To the contrary, I was always kept fully occupied with my supervisory duties, traffic matters and the Special Constabulary, in respect of whom I had overall control over their development and operational performance. I personally dealt with 20 fatal road traffic accidents over a period of two years, in other words 10 a year. Multiply that by the number of available inspectors on the division, around about eight, then the total deaths on just the major roads within the area stood at around 80 per year, a rather astounding and worrying statistic!

Of all the different duties I was engaged in during my time on Romford Division, three events stand out like a sore thumb above all else. All are connected to road traffic incidents and are undoubtedly indelibly transfixed into my memory because of the horrendous circumstances, emotional turmoil and life-changing consequences associated with them. In addition, each required a significant display of diplomacy and sensitivity.

(A). SOUTHBOUND A12, NORTH OF GALLOWS CORNER

I was the night duty duty officer covering the entire division when, at about 11.30pm, I was requested to attend the site of a road traffic accident in the offside (overtaking) southbound lane of the A12. On my arrival, officers had already started to divert moving traffic and were in the process of recording necessary details. It was clearly apparent that only two vehicles were involved and that the accident occurred as a direct result of a northbound vehicle crashing through the central reservation barrier and hitting a southbound car a glancing, but heavy, head on blow.

Damage to the south-facing car was restricted, primarily, to its front offside, which was badly crushed. The front windscreen was missing and there were no occupants in the vehicle. As I walked south along the A12, I saw a body lying in the road, approximately 20 yards ahead of me. I noticed that it was the lifeless body of a young female, which had been decapitated. That is not strictly an accurate description, since her skull had been 'pushed out' of the back of her head, leaving the skin of her face intact and attached to her body. As gruesome as it was, the fleshy remnant of the face, which was lying face-up on the ground, was still recognisable as that belonging to a young woman. I found the skull propped up against a support of the central reservation a few yards further on.

After completing all the necessary requirements at the scene, which included getting the ambulance service to convey the body to the local mortuary and establishing the identity of the young woman, I had the onerous task of visiting her home address, which was located in Hornchurch. There is no easy way to break such devastating news to loved ones and this case was no exception. I discovered that the victim was 19 years old, an only child, who had lived with her doting parents in Hornchurch since birth. Apparently, on the night in question she was returning home after a visit to her boyfriend. Understandably, her family, particularly her mother, were absolutely distraught with grief. Nevertheless, the mother was very insistent on wanting to accompany me to the mortuary to conduct the formal identification process for continuity purposes. In view of her daughter's appearance, I considered such action to be both inadvisable and inappropriate. However, it took all my powers of persuasion to dissuade her and get the father to perform the task. Conducting the formal identification and returning her personal effects was extremely hard on the father and he was visibly shaken and in a state of some shock by the time we finished. I escorted him back to his home address, but before I left him and his wife I contacted their local G.P. and made sure relatives were present to give them moral support and assistance. By the time I had completed my basic report, together with the practical issues associated with the accident, the night was almost over. Although I had not managed to take a break that night, I wasn't really too bothered as my appetite had deserted me for once and I felt physically and emotionally drained.

(B). HALL LANE, UPMINSTER – OUTSIDE UPMINSTER GOLF CLUB

On a night in September 1980, I was sitting quietly in Upminster Police Station doing some supervisory paper work when, just after midnight, I received a 'personal radio' call from one of my beat officers asking me to join him at Hall Lane, which was only a short distance away from my location, to assist with a potentially fatal road traffic accident (RTA). When I arrived at the site I couldn't believe my eyes, as I was presented with a scene of peace and tranquillity amongst mayhem and chaos. The area was completely devoid of pedestrians, onlookers (better known as 'rubber neckers') and motorists. Although the lack of vehicles was understandable, road block cordons having being implemented by my small team of officers at the scene, this didn't explain why such a normally busy residential area was deserted of humanity. This was particularly unusual, since an accident of this nature must have generated considerable noise and confusion!

For a stretch of about a hundred yards down Hall Lane, which was a pretty wide road, there was debris strewn all over the carriageway. Apart from an engine block, two seats and a wheel/tyre, which were spread about haphazardly in the road, there didn't appear to be anything else lying around of more than about six inches in diameter. It looked as though I had entered an extremely dishevelled scrap metal dealership. I quickly established that only two vehicles, a small utility van and a car, were involved in the accident; the causation factors were unknown at that time. The car was a three-wheeled Robin Reliant, whose chassis was composed entirely of fibreglass, which exploded like a grenade on impact.

The ambulance service, which had arrived prior to my attendance, had released the male driver and female passenger from their seats while they had been lying in the roadway and were conveying them to hospital, accompanied by the van driver. While peripheral tasks were being completed, I received a message informing me that the female passenger from the Robin Reliant had been pronounced dead on arrival at hospital. In order to maintain the continuity of identification for any subsequent court presentation, I immediately visited the hospital mortuary in company with the constable who had initially identified the female passenger to the ambulance crew. The deceased, who had suffered a broken neck, was a young female aged 22 years, who lived with her family, mum, dad and two brothers, in a detached property not more than half a dozen houses away from where the accident occurred. The driver of the Reliant, on the other hand, who was the deceased fiancée, had somehow managed miraculously to walk away from the accident with just a few abrasions and bruises. So far as the diver of the van was concerned, he sustained a twisted ankle and whiplash.

Irrespective of who was to blame for the accident, it must be anticipated that the deceased's fiancée would experience real difficulty coming to terms with the situation and interacting with her family in the future. However strong a character, living with his conscience is not going to be easy for the remainder of his life, even if he does seek professional physiological help. I found informing her parents of her death a monumental task, fringed with trepidation and some hesitation. The family were completely distraught and inconsolable, and at one point I thought they were all going to collapse, faint or have a fit, especially when they discovered the accident had occurred so close to where they lived. Fortunately, I had a women constable with me, who did a marvellous job getting the whole family back on an even keel. By the time I got the father to identify his daughter at the mortuary he was calm and rational.

Yet another full night's work for me, with a fair measure of stress and strain thrown in!

(C). WARLEY STREET (B186) ADJACENT TO A127

On a beautiful Sunday in June 1981, I was the early turn duty officer for Romford Division, looking forward to booking off duty and rejoining my family for a relaxing afternoon, when, at about 1pm, I got a 'personal radio message' seeking my attendance at a serious road traffic accident in a narrow county lane know as Warley Street located just off the A127 between Brentwood and Upminster. Of the many fatal accidents I had dealt with on Romford Division, this was by far the worst. Never before had I witnessed such carnage, it was truly staggering and not a little surreal. This was a multiple collision which had occurred in close proximity to a small humpbacked bridge, involving a total of five motor vehicles.

As I came down Warley Street from the A127, I drove down a fairly steep gradient towards the small humpbacked bridge before the road levelled out. Crumpled and twisted metal, together with other debris, littered the road around the bridge and surrounding embankments, and a number of people were wondering around aimlessly while others remained in their damaged vehicles. I noticed that there were a total of five vehicles involved in the accident: four cars and a motorcycle. One of the cars had been travelling south, while all the other vehicles had been going north in crocodile fashion. As I was only the second police officer to arrive on the scene and knew that I would also be the officer in overall charge, I immediately co-ordinated the assistance that would be required. I called for back-up from the Romford late-turn 'relief' personnel to cordon off Warley Street and divert traffic to other routes and assist me in conducting various tasks at the scene of the accident. I instructed traffic patrol officers to obtain all necessary technical specifications, including pertinent measurements, which may be required in any subsequent prosecution; called the ambulance service to attend to the injured; and finally I contacted a 'removal garage' to dispose of the vehicles involved. The various units arrived in what appeared to be double-quick time and commenced performing their respective functions impeccably, taking some elements of responsibility and pressure off my shoulders.

As I got closer to the scene of the accident I noticed there were a number of people moving around near the bridge but a short distance away from the vehicles, apparently in a daze, not fully cognisant of what was happening. I detailed some of my local officers who were present to contain these people in their respective groups to ensure medical treatment was administered as necessary, establish their individual roles in the accident, obtain their personal details and question them as potential witnesses. I saw an apparently lifeless body lying in the roadway next to the overturned motorcycle, while in the leading car there were two people in the front seat slumped in awkward positions, also not moving. In addition, there was another person slumped over the steering wheel of the car immediately behind the motorcyclist, which was the third vehicle in line.

As this accident was of such a complex and intricate nature, it would be helpful to the reader to be in possession of detailed background knowledge of how the accident occurred, in order to ascertain a clear picture of what transpired as the situation progressed.

One of the cars, a souped-up old Ford Cortina, with large thick rear-wheel tyres and smaller thinner front-wheel tyres, had been driven south down the hill in a southerly direction from the A127 towards the hump-back bridge, by its young male owner, accompanied by three teenage friends, two girls and a boy. He was showing off to his friends by driving too fast down the decline in Warley Street, but obviously realised his error prior to approaching the bridge, when he braked hard. Unfortunately, the adaptations and alterations to the suspension system and wheels of the Cortina significant reduced the reliability and effectiveness of the brakes and steering. As he braked, the car pulled sharply to the left, hitting the kerb. The driver then lost control and the car was suddenly then thrown in the air and veered to the right, into the path of the four oncoming vehicles travelling north towards the bridge. These vehicles were travelling close together at a slow speed as they entered the bridge in the order of car, motorcycle and two cars. While the Cortina was still in the air it ploughed almost head on into the first car, before striking the motorcyclist and coming back down to earth and hitting the offside front wing and door or the third car, which in turn pushed the rear of that car into the front of the fourth car.

When the ambulance paramedics arrived, they pronounced that the driver and female passenger in the front car were dead, as were the male motorcyclist and the male driver of the third car. Other than the four deceased, only two other people required hospital treatment. Any other injuries sustained were restricted to fairly minor cuts and bruises. Amazingly, the driver of the Cortina and his companions were injury free, albeit marginally shocked. As I was fully occupied at the scene and couldn't be released, I deferred responsibility for the identification of the deceased to two local officers, who accompanied the bodies to hospital and were present when they were formally identified by relatives. Saved the onerous task of informing family members of their loss, as they all resided beyond Romford Division, this problematic and difficult incident requiring considerable concentration and application, was exhausting to say the least. Bearing in mind I had already been on duty for nearly eight hours prior to being called to deal with the accident and that by the time I had performed all the requisite practical and administrative tasks associated with it, I had completed an additional eight hours of duty, I was pretty knackered both physically and mentally.

I felt so incensed about the circumstances surrounding the accident and how much devastation had been reaped on so many individuals and families by the sheer negligence of one person, however unintentional it may have been, that I completed a detailed 30-page report recommending that the driver of the Cortina should be prosecuted for the offence of 'causing death by dangerous driving'. My report was submitted to the Solicitors Department at N,S.Y. for due consideration. My recommendation was approved and the driver was summoned to appear before Chelmsford Crown Court. On the date of his appearance at court the defendant pleaded guilty to the offence and was sentenced to **two years disqualification from driving and a £500 fine.** While the court's decision was completely out of my control, I actually felt guilty and embarrassed as I was part of the legal profession which I felt at that time had implicated me in a miscarriage of justice. How anyone in their right mind, let alone a judge of the realm, could consider that the manslaughter of four people equated to a measly £500 fine and a two-year disqualification from driving, I will never understand. I felt, albeit I appreciate somewhat irrationally, that I had personally let the families of the deceased down. At that moment, I was quite disillusioned with our legal system, which I had so fervently defended on many occasions in the past as being fair and equitable. In my opinion, the law was quite definitely the proverbial **ASS** on this occasion.

BRIXTON RIOTS – April 1981

Located within the Borough of Lambeth is Brixton, a multi-racial neighbourhood where the difference between the 'haves and have-nots' was extremely noticeable during the early Eighties. It would be too easy to say it was simply a confrontation between police and young black youth born out of unrest fuelled by racial and social discord, as this would be a little too simplistic and misleading. During the late Seventies/early Eighties, social and economic deprivation, poor housing and high unemployment rates amongst the black Afro-Caribbean community within Brixton, had created frustration, suspicion and dissatisfaction in our social structure. As a consequence, a 'ghetto'-type atmosphere developed where 'street' crime (e.g. robberies, shoplifting, auto theft, assaults and drug offences) was increasing at an alarming rate. This generated more police activity in an effort to counter the growing problems but, as has proved to be the case in the past, it did little to resolve the predicament. To the contrary, all it tended to do was to promote a 'viscous circle'. Heightened police interest was, unfortunately, interpreted by black youth as systematic police harassment. The mistrust in the establishment and the police as its representative, was optimised by the 'flashpoint' incident giving rise to the riots; the police were actually assisting a black youth who had been stabbed by other black youths, when another group who witnessed the police intervention misinterpreted what was happening and attacked the police and released the stabbed youth.

As the inspector in charge of a fully trained and equipped 'public order' serial of 2 sergeants and 20 constables. Our equipment consisted of long transparent polycarbonate shields, dark-blue 'motorcycle'-type helmets, flame-retardant overalls, leather gloves and strong boots.

We arrived in Brixton late morning on the second day of the civil disturbances and were immediately sent to the rear of the police station on reserve. Passing through the vicinity, evidence of the previous day's troubles were all around us in the form of bricks and rubble strewn along the roads. Our first couple of hours proved to be pretty uneventful and boring, but as the afternoon progressed the situation deteriorated significantly. Some groups of black youths appeared to be well organised, engaging in systematic pre-planned attacks on police, while others were purely optimistic 'ad hoc' attacks on property and vehicles.

The first challenging deployment my unit was given was to the Atlantic Road and Coldharbour Lane areas, to assist patrol officers who had been separated from their colleagues. After de-bussing and organising the unit into its pro-active stance, we initially marched up Atlantic Road with our shields under our arms. However, this relaxed approach didn't last for long, as we were soon being bombarded by bricks and other missiles, which included Molotov cocktails (fire bombs). My officers managed to dodge or deflect the majority of the missiles thrown at them and rescue the few small groups of patrolling officers who had been separated from their own units. As we entered Coldharbour Lane, I saw an upturned Special Patrol Group (SPG) van across the pavement to our right, surrounded by local inhabitants; the officers from that van were nowhere to be seen. Again we came under sporadic attack from bricks and fire bombs, but apart from a few very minor abrasions, my unit was able to disburse those crowds they came into contact with without too much difficulty. On our return to Atlantic Road upon completion of our allocated task, we came across a small group of black youths in the process of looting a general store. Having been caught by surprise, my arresting officers were able to apprehend three offenders, who were then conveyed to the police station for processing.

Our second port of call was the main thoroughfare for the area, Brixton Road. On arrival, anyone would have been forgiven for thinking they were in a war zone. Rubble and all sorts of other debris covered the road and pavements, the glass windows of many of the shops had been smashed and motor vehicles were lying in unfamiliar positions, some on fire or badly damaged. My unit was required to perform foot-duty patrols for no other purpose than to dissuade further incidents of disorder and crime and to try, through overt policing, to return the area to some degree of normality. Once again, from time to time, we came under fire from missiles, but apart from scorching the right leg of my overalls after an amount of inflammable liquid from a fire bomb had managed to get under the bottom of my shield, no mishaps or injuries were sustained by members of my staff. My serial performed this rather monotonous task until about 9.30pm, when we were redeployed to the front of Brixton Police Station, where a large group of vociferous black youths were beginning to gather.

There was a genuine fear on the part of our senior command, that a concerted effort may be made by the demonstrators to storm the police station for the sole purpose of releasing their comrades from custody. My officers were used to bolster the strength of the cordon outside the front of the police station which, by the time we arrived, stood at about 10 rows deep. There was a lot of jostling, pushing and shoving, but this petered out fairly quickly, as there was insufficient room to get up to any other mischief. It didn't take long for the crowd to realise they were in a stalemate situation, by which time, the combination of dwindling interest and the lateness of the hour caused them to start disbursing from the area in droves. It was quite amazing how quickly the area went from utter confusion to virtual tranquillity.

Whilst not wishing to portray a sense of bravado, I can't remember feeling any fear or apprehension in connection with my duties at the Brixton riots. I readily accept that the situation as a whole was hair-raising, harrowing, threatening and exhausting, but I was so confident in the ability of my staff to deal with any eventuality in a positive and resolute manner, that I failed to contemplate any possible catastrophe. No doubt adrenalin played an important part in my overall perception, but I also felt committed and determined to play my part, as a patriotic citizen of my country, to help resolve any civil unrest.

AN INSUFFERABLE LITTLE MAN – April 1984

Shortly after the murder of W.P.C. Yvonne Fletcher outside the Libyan Embassy in St. James Square, London, I was sent to the location with a full serial of officers, to assist other units in setting up cordons at every entry/exit point into the square, in order to ensure the entire area surrounding the embassy was kept sterile. I had specific instructions not to let anyone into the Square, not even police officers, without appropriate authority from senior command at New Scotland Yard.

As the inspector in charge of the serial, I visited each of the cordons covered by my officers to ensure they were performing their duties correctly and were fully conversant with their responsibilities. While I was walking between two different locations, I received a radio message from one of my officers at a Jermyn Street cordon, stating he was having difficulty with a member of the press who was demanding entry into the square as he had an appointment to interview an official from the Libyan Embassy. I informed my constable that I would immediately make my way to his location to deal with the situation and that in the meantime he was not to permit anyone access to the area.

As I arrived at the cordon, I was suddenly approached by a very irate, short, ginger-haired man who was waving his finger in front of my face demanding entry into St James Square. When I declined his request he almost lost control of his emotions and said, "Don't you know who I am?"

In reply I said, "Should I, sir?"

Unfortunately, my response went down like a lead balloon and he introduced himself rather officiously as, "I'm Nicholas Whitchell, a senior political reporter. I need to interview an embassy official." When I informed him that I would check with my superiors to confirm with whom he had an appointment, he became defensive and even more aggressive and eventually acknowledged that he did not have a fixed appointment with anyone, but was hoping to be able to obtain an interview.

He didn't talk to me, he talked at me, as if I was some insignificant low life that he could barely bring himself to communicate with. Mr. Whitchell was abusive throughout our contact, threatening to impede my future career in the Service and stating he would be lodging a formal complaint about my behaviour. There are not many people I have met in my life who I have taken an instant dislike to, but he was certainly an exception. I found him to be an arrogant, insignificant little man with ideas well above his station. If I had been a qualified psychologist, I would probably have assessed him as being someone with an inferiority complex about his stature, or should I say lack of it. I am convinced he thought he was of superior intellect and gained a lot of pleasure from talking down to people and trying to belittle them.

Once he realised he was getting nowhere with me he turned on his heels and walked away muttering to himself. It did come to my notice that he made further attempts to get through other cordons, but with no more success than he had trying to get past me. An insufferable little man describes him to a tee and if I never meet him again then that would be too soon!

COAL MINERS' STRIKE – 1984/1985

The coal miners' strike is worthy of receiving a mention in these memoirs, not for any remarkable or outstanding occurrence, but because it represented a pivotal period in the political history of the United Kingdom, in respect of which I was directly involved. It was an industrial dispute on a truly monumental scale. A lot has already been written about the miners' strike, but hopefully I can add a little more from a ground-level perspective to enhance the readers' appreciation of both sides of the equation. In public order terms it was unparalleled, not for ferocity, but for sheer scale and duration. In essence, it was a dispute by hard-line, left-wing political activists led by the president of the National Union of Miners, Mr. Arthur Scargill, in an attempt to bring down the Conservative Government of the day, the prime minister of which was a very astute woman named Margaret Thatcher.

While there were hard-line factions within the mining fraternity, I found the vast majority of miners to be honest, hardworking and down to earth people who had little or no interest in getting involved in violent confrontation. Having policed many of the picket lines at different collieries during the dispute, the miners came over as genuine, good humoured and rational individuals who shunned intimidation or civil disorder. While they were cajoled into going on strike in the first instance on the pretext of saving their industry and preserving jobs, it didn't take long before most miners realised that the true objectives were politically orientated.

The ultimate failure of the miners' strike was as much down to the determination of the prime minister, Mrs. Thatcher, as it was to the miners themselves. Suffice to say, that during the period of the strike when I performed duty at many of the collieries, I never encountered any real unpleasantness. I appreciate there were certain locations where violent disorder did arise, but most of those were restricted to known pockets of political descent.

MURDER OF P.C. BLAKELOCK – BROADWATER FARM –
October 1985

On 6th October 1985, I was the senior late duty officer (chief inspector) on 'G' District when, at about 6pm, I was instructed to provide a full contingent of officers from my area and report with them to Tottenham Police Station. On arrival, we were deployed on short foot patrols around the periphery of the Broadwater Farm Council Estate, where indiscriminate disturbances had been ongoing throughout the afternoon.

Once again, this type of residential property controlled by Local Authorities, epitomised the problems faced by inner-city areas during the 1970s to 1980s. As with all the other riots I have had the dubious pleasure of being involved in during my police service, the initial incident giving rise to the 'lighting of the blue touch paper' at Broadwater Farm, had absolutely no bearing or relevance on the real reasons behind the public discontent and disorder. In reality, as has been the case with other major public disorder events, it was an accumulation of a number of factors, not least of which were: social/economic deprivation, poor quality housing and high unemployment, accompanied by suspicion and mistrust of authority.

As darkness descended on the estate, the frequency and level of violence intensified alarmingly. Large groups of black youths were observed marauding around the blocks of flats, as well as within stairwells and connecting walkways. They appeared to be well organised and co-ordinated, but this could have been a bit of an overstatement, bearing in mind that, as local residents, they would have had comprehensive knowledge of the layout of the entire estate. Police officers were beginning to get injured left, right and centre irrespective of the protective equipment they were wearing. Was this spontaneous disorder; no way. To the contrary, in my opinion, it was calculated and pre-meditated on an unprecedented scale. I have no doubt that the agenda for the main protagonists was anarchy and nothing less. While pursuing their objective, they took advantage of the confusion and fear that had been generated by also engaging in looting, arson and damage to property. Unfortunately, radical factions within the black community latched on to the left wing 'media tag' of police being 'institutionally racist' to justify their own abysmal behaviour.

Owing to heightened tension and the increased regularity of attacks on police, my entire serial of one inspector, two sergeants and 20 constables was deployed within the Broadwater Farm Estate by mid-evening, performing high-profile foot patrols. Our primary function was to dissuade others from joining the mayhem and disbursing those we came in contact with who were in the process of causing trouble. While patrolling close to one of the blocks of flats, I saw a large group of black youths gathered together jostling each other; while close to this group I could see a few police officers struggling with something on the ground. As the officers appeared to be in some difficultly, I instructed half my unit to follow me to the scene immediately, while the remainder were to provide protection to our rear.

As I got closer to the mob, I could see that many of the black youths were engaged in violent behaviour, by thrashing and striking out at people in close proximity and throwing missiles. I also saw two officers pulling away from the crowd, dragging a fellow officer along the ground, who appeared to be unconscious. I immediately deployed some of my officers to render assistance and provide safe cover for their exit from the scene. As they passed my position, I could tell that the officer being dragged along the ground, who I now know to have been P.C. Keith Blakelock, was in a very bad way; he subsequently died from his injuries. I could see he had numerous facial and chest wounds and did not appear to be cognisant of anything around him. At this time, my team of officers came under a sustained missile attack. I can only describe it as a brutal and frenzied onslaught during which a number of my officers, including myself, were struck on the head and body with an assortment of masonry, metal objects and bottles. I am extremely thankful for the 'Nato'-style helmet I was wearing at the time, which undoubtedly saved me from sustaining serious head injuries. Upon my directions, once we had ensured the safe departure of the ambulance paramedics with P.C. Blakelock, my serial re-grouped and made a tactical withdrawal back towards our transport. The crowd of black youths pursuing my serial broke away and vanished into the shadows before we could manage to regain the offensive. At the conclusion of this encounter with the rampaging mob, I don't believe there was a single member of my team who had not received some form of minor injury. Nevertheless, not a single one of them left the unit for medical treatment while we were on duty. For the remainder of the evening we were pushed from pillar to post, reacting to whatever arose. However, by the early hours of the 7th, the police had managed to regain complete control of the estate, largely due to the fact that the majority of black youth had by then lost enthusiasm and interest in their cause and had vanished back into the 'woodwork'!

Prior to being dismissed from duty, I was directed to report to Tottenham Police Station to perform de-briefing and counselling duties for officers from other divisions prior to their release from Broadwater Farm. I can't remember ever seeing so many 'shell-shocked' officers in one place before. The brutality and ferocity of the attacks perpetrated against them was so intense that without their bravery, discipline, comradeship and strong sense of duty, I have no doubt many would have been bludgeoned into submission. In addition, many of those who I interviewed were members of the 'walking wounded', as they carried nasty injuries inflicted by many different means, including both knives and firearms, which had not, up to that time, received any medical treatment. Many of the officers were clearly traumatised by their experiences and could not believe the concentrated viciousness or assorted weaponry that had been directed at them. Whilst I suppose I should not have been surprised to see so many officers looking so dishevelled and bedraggled after such a gruelling and demanding tour of duty, their dejected demeanour spoke volumes.

While I found the Broadwater Farm riots very frightening and traumatic at the time, I don't think I had any residual problems. The death of P.C. Blakelock was a sad, sad day for the Metropolitan Police Service, but it was yet another reminder never to take anything for granted. Unfortunately, as always seems to be the case when public disorder occurs, police involvement attracts criticism from certain sections of the press. It appears that the old adage 'damned if you do, damned if you don't' is pretty accurate! On this occasion, I not only felt the criticism was unjustified but that it also, to some extent, diluted the true nature of the riots and the abhorrence of P.C. Blakelock's murder.

PARTYING AROUND HACKNEY – 1986

To highlight the following example is probably a little unfair, as it is but one of many similar jobs I completed during the busy year that was 1986. In my capacity as chief inspector 'operations' for Hackney Division, it was my specific responsibility to co-ordinate and execute all search warrants relating to premises where it was alleged illegal gaming or liquor-licensing offences were being committed. For no discernible or logical reason, illegal drinking clubs, better known as 'Shebeens', were an extremely popular leisure facility in Hackney, especially amongst the Afro-Caribbean community. Shebeens were basically entrepreneurial ventures run by unscrupulous individuals keen on making a 'quick buck'. Premises adapted for the purpose usually consisted of a large room with inadequate lighting and limited furniture and fixtures. Offences under the Licensing Acts were purely 'summary', meaning there was no power of arrest. Additionally, it was only those people organising or running illegal drinking establishments for profit who committed an offence. However, the most powerful weapon in the battle to prevent and stop the sale of unlicensed liquor is the search warrant. It bestows authority to detain and seize all alcoholic beverages found at illegal sales, with the strong possibility of an order being made for its complete destruction.

Information came into my possession alleging that certain premises in Martello Street, E8 were being used to host the illegal sale of intoxicating liquor. I arranged for a sergeant and constable to conduct plain clothes observations on the suspected premises on two consecutive Fridays for the specific purpose of determining whether or not the premises were being used to sell unlicensed alcohol, to obtain a detailed layout of the premises and to identify who was organising/running the operation. My officers confirmed that, not only was unlicensed alcohol being sold, but customers were also being charged a fee to enter the premises. In addition, the organisers were identified and all other pertinent details obtained which satisfied me that a police operation would be justified. Accordingly, I instructed my 'plain clothes' sergeant to attend the local magistrates court and apply for a search warrant.

A week later at 10pm, I had a team of uniform officers, who I intended to use as the raiding party, assembled in the canteen at Hackney Police Station for the purpose of giving them a detailed briefing. The briefing incorporated the purpose of the raid, what could reasonably be expected upon entry and, more importantly, the allocation of specific roles and responsibilities. The three sergeants and 30 constables who were available were assigned the following designated roles: **one sergeant plus two constables – deal solely with the seizure, listing and removal of all liquor found on the premises; three constables – to assist in the transportation of any prisoners to the police station by police van; two constables – security duties to control entry and egress to premises; 20 constables – 10 teams of two officers to interview and record details of the clientele; two constables – to collect, bag and deposit at the police station all items discarded on the premises (e.g. offensive weapons and drugs); one sergeant – general supervision of interview teams; and one sergeant – chief inspector's administrative assistant.** Upon completion of the briefing, the entire raiding party was sent in convoy to a location close to the venue where they remained on standby awaiting a pre-arranged signal from the observation team, indicating that the raid was 'GO'.

Shortly after arriving at the standby point, the observation officers, who were ensconced inside the premises acquiring evidence for a future prosecution, signalled that all was ready for our entry. The entire team, with me leading from the rear, entered the premises from the only entrance into the property and went down a short flight of stairs into a large, poorly lit room with a few chairs bordering the perimeter walls. All my officers quickly departed to their designated positions and commenced their duties. On entering the premises, there was a deafening sound of 'reggae' music emanating from a large sound system, accompanied by a thick, yellowy smoke hanging in the air, which it was felt could be cut with a knife. This 'smog', which stank of cannabis, probably because it was cannabis, or should I say the by-product of smoking that drug, quickly dissipated once the entrance to the make-shift club was kept open. Once the initial shock and surprise over our entry had passed, all went deathly quiet as the music was turned off and the cacophony of sound produced by the patrons suddenly ceased. It was quite amusing really, because when total silence reigned, I quite clearly heard the sound of clinks and clanks as items fell to the floor discarded by their owners. I immediately introduced myself to the organiser, produced and showed him the search warrant and then started to obtain his full particulars and question him. He was subsequently subjected to individual face-to-face confrontations with all drinking customers, cautioned and shown the alcoholic drink found on the premises. This alcohol, which was seized and confiscated, formed the basis of the 'summons' application for the unlicensed sale of intoxicating liquor. At the conclusion of the raid, a large quantity of different beers (40 crates), wines (120 bottles) and spirits (80 bottles), were seized and taken into police custody for safe keeping pending future directions from the local magistrates court. Four people were separately arrested for drug-related offences; a quantity of drugs in plastic bags and silver foil were found abandoned on the floor of the premises, together with an assortment of knives and knuckledusters.

This raid subsequently led to a successful prosecution and directions being issued by the court for the entire consignment of confiscated contraband to be destroyed. In line with the court's instructions, the observation officers, in my presence, poured the entire stock of beers, wines and spirits down the drain in the rear courtyard of Hackney

Police Station. The task took about two hours to complete and caused some mild amusement amongst other staff passing through the police station yard. Additionally, the smell of alcohol permeated throughout the yard for many days, which turned a few visitors' heads as they passed the drain. During my time as chief inspector 'operations' on Hackney Division, I gained a bit of a reputation, both internally and externally, for successfully prosecuting unlicensed drinking establishments. Consequently, the number of illegal drinking houses within the borough dropped significantly.

BITE NIGHT AND FLIGHT – 1986

One Saturday evening in June 1986, while engaged in senior duty officer functions on Hackney Division, my attendance was requested at Dalston Police Station. On arrival, the local 'duty' inspector approached me and introduced his newly promoted uniform superintendent, who was based at Stoke Newington. I was told that later that same evening a 'drugs search warrant' was to be executed by the superintendent, together with a dedicated raiding party, at premises known as the 'Four Aces Club'. I was asked if I would be prepared to remain in the background as an observer to give advice if and when requested to do so.

This licensed drinking/dance club, located in Dalston Road near the junction with Ashwin Street, was an establishment frequented by Afro-Caribbeans, renowned for its connection with illegal drug use. It was also known to be a highly volatile location, a 'tinder box' which could go up at a moment's notice, if not handled carefully and sensitively. It was also necessary to ensure that sufficient officers were available to complete the task with ease, as any weakness would be pounced upon quickly.

I attended the superintendent's briefing and was impressed with how comprehensive it was, but I was somewhat concerned over his intended use of 'dog handlers' to suppress any potential disorder. To some extent, he was gambling on the rumour that Afro-Caribbeans were uncomfortable around dogs, particularly ones with large teeth and a grumpy disposition! However, working with dogs in very close proximity to people in confined spaces, irrespective of how well trained they were, was fraught with danger.

As the raid unfolded, I was standing to the rear of the police contingent looking at a dog handler and his Alsatian, who were stationary directly behind the uniform superintendent. As everyone moved forward in a sort of crocodile line to reach their designated positions without delay within the club premises, the foyer suddenly emptied, leaving the superintendent alone with the dog handler behind him and a rather excited dog on a leash. Suddenly, I saw the dog lunge forward open his mouth and clamp his jaws shut over the superintendent's left buttock; it seemed to happen in slow motion. I heard a sharp cry of pain and then, like greased lightning, the young superintendent shot past me holding his left buttock in his left hand, heading for the police station on foot; that was the last I saw of him that evening. I returned to the Four Aces Club where news of the dog bite had preceded me and found that the police operation was in the capable hands of the duty inspector.

Some may well say that the above events amounted to summary justice. I can't help having a bit of a wry smile on my face when thinking about it, particularly since I did provide him with words of caution about the use of a dog immediately after his briefing. I later discovered that although the flesh had not been broken, six indentation bruise marks were left in the superintendent's posterior. I wonder if he ever worked with dogs again from 'behind'!

WAPPING PRINT DISPUTE, NEWS INTERNATIONAL – 1986/1987

For the best part of a year, while still chief inspector 'operations' for Hackney, I was seconded to Leman Street Police Station to assist with the policing of the Wapping print dispute. On alternate weeks, I performed the internal role of 'controller' and the external role of 'sector operations commander'. As 'controller', I had responsibility, together with a small communications team, for the assessment, allocation and distribution of all police resources in order to ensure demonstrations were conducted in an orderly and law-abiding manner. So far as the position of 'sector operations commander' was concerned, I had supervisory responsibility for the deployment and actions of those officers within my sector.

This internal dispute between print workers and owners proved to be a milestone in the relationship between the trade unions and proprietors. Industrial relations had been deteriorating for many years owing to the 'closed-shop' approach adopted by the workers, where they were not prepared to introduce modern processes, practices or technology. The aim of the strikers was to block and disrupt the distribution of Murdock's newspapers. However, this objective proved to be an abject failure thanks to the success of the police in maintaining the freedom of movement of all transport frequenting News International.

While the vast majority of print workers were decent, honest, rational and reasonable people, who had absolutely no interest in misbehaviour, there was a determined 'hardcore' of troublemakers from the 'nutters rent a crowd'. These vitriolic and unpredictable activists who, in reality, probably had little or no connection with the print industry, were not averse to engaging in violent disorder and intimidation. I was personally involved on a number of occasions when police officers were subjected to violent attacks from an assortment of missiles, including pieces of concrete, bricks, Molotov cocktails, bottles, lamp posts and wooden staves. Many police officers were injured during these horrendous, vicious confrontations, but they responded, in my opinion, in a manner equitable to defending themselves and restoring public tranquillity. As appears to be the norm, police were accused by some members of the media of using excessive force and abusing civil liberties. However, now that many years have passed and the dust has well and truly settled, it may well be considered that the police were neither disproportionate nor misdirected in their actions!

Sustaining or intensifying the dispute on a day-to-day, week-to-week and month-to-month basis, proved to be an impossible and futile task, as the energy and determination of the strikers was slowly sapped and neutralised. Eventually, having failed to achieve anything constructive, the dispute ended following exhaustion and demoralisation on the part of the print workers. The strikers were not the only ones who were the worse for wear. After working 12-hour days for almost a year, with little family life and barely a day off, I was in desperate need of some 'rest and relaxation'.

(A). JUST A LITTLE NIBBLE – NEIGH

One busy evening, probably a Wednesday, since Saturdays and Wednesdays tended to be the days of greatest activity at the Wapping print dispute, I was performing the role of 'sector operations commander', when I became aware that a large group of demonstrators at Wellclose Square had broken away from the main body of 'static' protesters and were walking, on mass, east along the back streets parallel to the News International premises. Being suspicious of their motives, I detailed a full serial of uniform constables to follow them on foot and keep their movements under close scrutiny.

For about an hour, this cat and mouse process continued up, down and along various local roads without any specific purpose being identified. However, as I believed it was the intention of the demonstrators to surreptitiously get behind police lines in an attempt to enter News International property, I had my officers maintain close contact with the opposition in an effort to deter them from such an activity or from engaging in any indiscriminate disorder involving violence or criminal damage.

All of a sudden, the demonstrators broke up into three distinct factions and moved away in different directions like a starburst. I split my officers accordingly, but this left me seriously short of resources should any pressure be brought to bear at a wide thoroughfare.

I stayed in situ at The Highway, a central location, listening for progress reports from those members of my staff who followed each of the three groups, to determine the desirability, or otherwise, of deploying 'reserve' personnel at short notice to shore up any gaps in police-cordon potential.

Within a relatively short period of time, I was told that one of the bands of demonstrators had turned into Dellow Street, a wide road, and was travelling south back towards The Highway. However, more importantly, the demonstrators were becoming more vociferous and agitated, which was a disturbing sign. I decided it would be prudent to place a police cordon across Dellow Street, thereby denying access into The Highway. I called for the assistance of Mounted Branch to help in the completion of this task, as it would only need a relatively small number of horses and riders, in comparison with a large contingent of foot constables, to perform the same function.

I immediately went to the location where I decided on the precise spot for the cordon before deploying six mounted officers with their horses across the road interspersed with foot-duty constables. Seeing their way effectively blocked by police horses was obviously a little like 'a red rag to a bull', as it goaded many in the crowd into becoming more vitriolic and combative. I stood on the nearside (left) pavement close to the first horse in the cordon, ready to provide directions should the cordon come under attack. All of a sudden, I noticed a few brave souls from the crowd rush forward ahead of their colleagues. One of these, a man in his late twenties, who was average in every other way, appeared to be rushing towards me, but before he reached me, I managed to dodge out of his way. However, I was taken aback when he ignored me and stopped directly in front of the first horse in the line and quite deliberately swung his right arm back and then punched the horse with full force squarely in the snout. Initially, the horse whinnied and started to shy away, but then responded by opening its mouth and giving the demonstrator a good, firm nip on his left arm. Before any of my officers could arrest him for cruelty to animals, he had dashed back into the throng, holding his arm shouting in pain, where he then vanished.

In retrospect, the bite by the horse was undoubtedly a swifter, more effective and memorable piece of justice than had the man been taken to court, where he would probably have been sentenced to a 'conditional discharge'.

(B). CRASH, BANG, WALLOP – WHOOPS!

Late on a Saturday evening, I was on my way to Ensign Street, in company with a serial of 'public order' trained officers who were fully equipped with 'shields', in answer to a call from the 'police control room' to serious disorder by a rampaging mob. Ensign Street was close to the main entrance of News International and the static demonstration area for the Wapping print dispute. On our arrival at the entrance to the location by The Highway, I saw a considerable amount of debris strewn in the roadway, but no sign of revellers although there was plenty of noise further up the road out of sight! The rubble consisted of bricks, masonry, glass and chunks of wood. As a precautionary measure, I instructed the officers to de-bus and proceed up Ensign Street in formation with shields at the ready.

The conditions facing us were almost indescribable and overwhelming, as the road was a virtual bomb site. As I advanced up the road, I saw numerous seriously damaged motor vehicles parked against the nearside kerb. We were suddenly confronted by a group of about 40 pretty hostile protesters, many of whom were in possession of an assortment of missiles.

Although marked by verbal rhetoric and threatening postures, there was a virtual 'strand off' for about 10 minutes while both sides assessed their respective positions and options. While they outnumbered the police by two to one, it is probable that the demonstrators considered that they may have bitten off more than they could chew by facing a team of highly trained and equipped 'public order' officers. On the other hand, I had to consider the possible success of disbursing this violent group of protestors without sustaining heavy casualties amongst my staff. The decision was taken out of my hands by subsequent events.

After a brief respite, some of the more resilient and provocative protestors rushed towards the front line of shield officers and hurled their missiles indiscriminately in their direction. At the time, I was standing on the left side of my unit, between their front line and a number of cars parked against the nearside pavement. I was paying particular attention to a young man in his late teens, who was getting uncomfortably close to my position, carrying what was subsequently identified as a large broken part of a concrete lamp post. Before reaching me, he let fly with his piece of lamp post, but its trajectory was clearly way off target. It veered to the right, flew over my head and the officer's behind me and then, as if in slow motion, ploughed into the bonnet of a silver BMW parked against the kerb. After bouncing off the bonnet of the car, it ploughed and smashed into the front windscreen, destroyed the steering wheel assembly, and came to rest impaled in the driver's seat. After discharging his missile, the youth rushed back to his colleagues and took up his original position next to a middle-aged man, who turned to him and appeared to have a brief heated discussion with him.

Following the violent onslaught, I immediately dispatched my entire unit to forcibly dismantle and disburse the crowd before they could re-group and organise themselves again. Because they were packed too close together, my officers were also able to arrest the main protagonist before they could evade capture. Included in the arrests were the youth who chucked the lamp post and the older man who had been standing next to him.

As the older man was escorted past me, he must have noticed the insignia of my rank and realised I was a senior officer, because he turned to me and expressed the view that it was definitely not his day as he had only attended the 'rally' to support his young nephew who was a print worker and that he was unwittingly pulled along by the momentum and atmosphere generated by the demonstrators, which he could not extricate himself from. Additionally, he stated he had been arrested mistakenly and that to put the proverbial cherry on the cake, his nephew had managed to effectively destroy his BMW that had been parked in Ensign Street.

To be honest, I initially felt genuinely sorry for the elder man, who had clearly had a bad day. However, my compassion was quickly quenched when I was informed that he had been arrested in possession of a Molotov cocktail. Would this be a case of the end justifying the muddle?

BRAMSHILL POLICE COLLEGE, HAMPSHIRE – January/June 1989

Bramshill Police College is a national institution catering, predominantly, for the higher managerial and leadership training of potential senior managers within the Police Service throughout the United Kingdom. The courses, which are devised and implemented at different operational and administrative levels, are normally undertaken on a residential basis of varying lengths. Apart from learning legal skills, they provided students with an ideal opportunity to gain a better understanding of procedures and practices adopted by the numerous different Constabularies (43 during my service) policing this country.

Time spent in this college environment was interesting, absorbing, thought provoking and challenging, together with being competitive, particularly in connection with organised sporting activities. Like most disciplined organisations, rules and regulations were part of everyday life and the college was no exception. The most important rule, which had to be followed without exception, related to standard of dress. All officers were expected to dress immaculately in their respective uniforms from breakfast time to until the conclusion of dinner. Although I had attended three courses at Bramshill during my police career, the two following examples are from my third and final six-month residential course, the Intermediate Command Course. This was a very demanding and high-powered period of training, geared towards the most senior ranks within the Service.

(A). A BURNING RING OF FIRE

On a rare mid-week evening when I had no research, revision or preparation to do for a presentation the flowing day, three friends from my class and I decided to forgo our college dinner in favour for an Indian 'Ruby Murray' at a local restaurant in Hook. Being a bit of a curry connoisseur and a lover of food, I considered it was about time I put my money where my mouth was and take the plunge by trying the hottest curry available for human consumption, the 'PHALL'. When taking my order, I vividly remember the waiter saying to me, "Are you really sure sir, it's very very hot?" Albeit a little reticent after his words of caution, I, nevertheless, foolishly stuck to my original order. To make me feel a little better, however, I also ordered a nice cold pint of larger.

Understandably, the very appealing pint of larger was served well in advance to the meal, which was a great shame as it had to stand untouched until I had finished eating. I had learnt long ago that drinking a cold liquid while eating a curry was definitely a no no, as it only exacerbated any discomfort you were already feeling. Initially, I was quite pleased with myself, as for the first four or five minutes there were no adverse feelings; boy should I have kept my thoughts to myself! In no time at all, my lips and mouth started to go numb and tingly, my nose started to drip and go numb, my ears felt like they were on fire with steam shooting out them and my eyes were stinging and watering profusely. All in all, I felt distinctly uncomfortable and my head really didn't feel as though it belonged to my body. I managed to finish the phall and although it would be a lie to say I thoroughly enjoyed the experience, in some perverse way it was a success as I had managed to achieve a long-time goal. However, in retrospect it may have been a better option to have partaken in the college dinner! Nevertheless, I thoroughly enjoyed my pint of lager, which went down my throat in about four large swigs which didn't touch the sides of my gullet. After finishing my drink, things seemed to return to normal pretty quickly and by the time we got back to the college, I felt content and ready for a good night's sleep.

Part two of this saga, for that's exactly what it was, was when I woke the following morning with a compelling urge to visit the toilet. As I went to sit down on the loo seat I must have had a premonition of things to come, as I was suddenly taken by a very uncomfortable sensation in my nether region. Instead of sitting on the seat, I maintained a 'hovering position' above the bowl and let it all hang out. As the world exploded below me and my bum and 'ring piece' (anus for the uninitiated) gave vent to their disapproval by providing me with excruciating pain, numbness and general discomfort in that order, the words of that iconic song by the country singer Johnny Cash *'The burning ring of fire'* came flooding back to my mind. When I finally departed from the toilet about a half an hour later, I felt bow-legged and weak-kneed, sensations which remained with me for the better part of that day. It goes without saying that I have stayed well away from the phall curry ever since. Should I ever be tempted to suggest having one anytime in the future, whoever is with me has my permission to have me 'sectioned' under the Mental Health Act provisions!

(B). GOOD LUCK OR JUST A FOWL MESS

As explained earlier, all students were expected to be smartly dressed in full uniform during class times. One morning while making my way to breakfast down the pathway from my accommodation block to the canteen restaurant, minding my own business, I felt a firm thud on my left shoulder. Looking down, I realised that I had been defecated upon from a great height by one of those winged giants called a Canadian goose, which gathered in their thousands on the college grounds. Being shat upon from such a height, the poop just exploded on impact and spread down the front of my tunic.

The bird shit was of a soft consistency, green and white in colour, which didn't exactly tone in with my blue tunic. To the contrary, it made me look extremely scruffy and unpresentable. I had no option but to return to my room and change into my spare jacket, which meant I missed breakfast. In the circumstances, I felt rather peeved and fed up although I suppose I should have been thankful and relieved for small mercies, in that I didn't look up when the goose deposited its load or I might have unwittingly volunteered for a 'veggie' breakfast!

COMMUNITY LIAISON OFFICER, 'G' DISTRICT –1989/1991

I was personally selected for this post by my area assistant commissioner, so it would have been career suicide for me to reject it. While I was not disappointed with the role in itself, it meant having to return yet again to the Borough of Hackney, where I had already served for a number of years.

While I completed many important tasks successfully during my tenure as the community liaison officer, the example that stands out in my mind above all else is probably the least important and most insignificant, but it could have had far-reaching effects and caused considerable embarrassment to both myself and the Service had I fallen for the trap that one of our local politicians was underhandedly trying to set me up for. Resorting to 'dirty tricks' is not something a so-called honest politician should be proud of, but I'm certain that had she achieved her ends, she would have gladly taken great pleasure in milking it for all that it was worth.

Under the rules of Sec.106 of the Police and Criminal Evidence Act, a senior police officer on every borough was required to attend meetings involving local councillors. Prior to one such meeting, I received information from a friendly councillor, that I was going to be asked a question by a certain female MP on how many black youths in comparison with their white colleagues, were stopped and searched within the Borough of Hackney, with the ultimate intention of putting me in a corner and having me admit, even if by implication alone, that police action was racially prejudiced. As a consequence, I did some research on the subject and discovered that 60% of stops in the borough were performed on black youths in comparison with only 40% on white youths. However, this was far from disproportionate since the local community in the borough at that time consisted of 70% blacks, 20% whites and 10% other denominations. I attended the meeting armed with this data and when asked the question by the smug female MP I gave the information I had obtained. She was visibly shocked at being stopped in her tracks, but from that point on, I gained her respect and never had any further trouble from her. She was clearly aware of the comparison between the number of stops against black and white youths prior to the meeting, but hadn't, in her excitement, delved deep enough to find out the other information I provided which put the matter into perspective.

Regrettably, at this juncture it would be unwise for me to name the politician concerned, as she is still very much a strong influence in the current Labour Party and shadow cabinet. Save to say, she is a divisive bitch of the first order who I wouldn't trust any further than I could throw her. Nevertheless, I learnt one valuable lesson out of this particular sordid affair and that was that being a policeman in the modern era just wasn't enough, you also had to be politically astute.

PLAISTOW DIVISION, 'K' DISTRICT – 1991/1995

In 1991, after spending a large portion of my police career at different ranks and roles in the Borough of Hackney, I applied for a transfer to Newham as soon as I saw a vacancy arise on Plaistow Division for the deputy divisional commander's role. Fortunately, my application proved successful and within two years, when my boss retired on age limit, I was promoted in situ to A/chief superintendent and took over as the divisional commander.

In addition to the normal duties undertaken by divisional commanders, I also had overall responsibility for devising and implementing the policing arrangements in connection with the Premiership football club, West Ham United, which fell within the jurisdiction of Plaistow Division. During my five-season association with the club, I experienced many different emotions and sensations attributed to dealing with large crowds in a 'sport' public-order environment. Most were cordial, albeit demanding, whilst others were distinctly frightening and dangerous, particularly when dealing with West Ham versus Millwall F.C. hooligans. During my period of tenure, it was pleasing to note that the volume of hooliganism had reduced to a trickle, largely due to the introduction of highly trained plain-clothes police spotters, although I'm sure that the emergence of all seater stands also played an important part in the reduction of violent confrontation at football grounds.

The most remarkable memory I have, and one which will stay with me and be treasured for the rest of my life, occurred at the conclusion of the last game of the season in May 1995, against Manchester United F.C., before I moved on to pastures new. While de-briefing my staff in the Police Control Room after the match, I was approached by Mr. Harry Redknapp, the West Ham F.C. manager and escorted to the Directors' Lounge situated on the first floor of the West Stand. On entry, I saw it was packed with celebrities, senior executives from the club and most of the first team players. Harry handed over to the club chairman, Mr. Terence Brown who, standing next to me, made a short speech thanking me for my commitment and assistance to West Ham F.C. When he finished, Sir Bobby Charlton presented me with a whisky decanter and a set of glasses inscribed with the 'Hammers' motif. This presentation was most unexpected and the gift now has pride of place in one of my glass display cabinets at home.

2 AREA NORTH-EAST 'OPERATIONS' – 1995/1997

Towards the latter part of 1995, I was formally promoted to the rank of chief superintendent and given the largest and most prestigious command available on 2 Area, that of O.C.U. commander 2 Area North-East 'operations'. The primary purpose of the combined units under my command; the Dog Section, Mounted Branch, Traffic Section and Territorial Support Group (TSG – shield-trained officers), was to provide support and assistance to all divisions on 2 Area.

When including administrative civil staff, there were approximately 400 personnel under my direct responsibility, together with an annual budget of £30 million. Because of the size and distribution of my resources, I had two separate offices, one at the Bow TSG Base and the other, my main office, at the Chadwell Heath Traffic Unit. Given my supervisory responsibilities, it was incumbent on me to visit those police officers under my command on a fairly regular basis. As they were spread over a vast area, this entailed a considerable amount of travel on my part. Of the many incidents, experiences and events that I was a part of while O.C.U. commander before my retirement from the Service in November 1997, three stand out more vividly than any of the others, regrettably, not for the best of reasons.

(A). A BIG DROP FOR A LITTLE COP – OUCH !

One of the more pleasant and relaxing tasks I performed, was welcoming new officers joining units under my command and attending the start and/or passing out parades for divisional officers undertaking courses provided by my staff. One such occasion was when the Traffic Section inspector asked me to formally open a Standard Motorcycle Course for newly selected traffic officers, utilising the motorcycle currently in service at that time, the BMW R80RT, a very large heavy machine. On entering the enclosed garage area, where officers normally received their mechanical and maintenance training, I saw five officers dressed in their motorcycle equipment standing next to their respective machines, which were on their main stands, with the sergeant instructor in the lead position.

Of the five trainees who were present, I noticed that one was a young woman constable (W.P.C.). My attention was drawn to her because I recall thinking just how short she was in relation to the BMW motorcycle she was standing next to. In fact, she was of very slight build and couldn't have been more than 5' 4" tall. My instincts told me there was absolutely no chance, even with the best will in the world, that she would make the grade and pass the course. This had everything to do with brawn and nothing to do with brain. While I realised that the Service was determined to display its full commitment to equal opportunities, I failed to comprehend how anyone in their right mind, however well intentioned, could seriously consider this particular W.P.C. as a suitable candidate for Traffic Division based on her physical prowess. Apart from the physical restrictions, there would also be a real risk of injury to the officer herself.

The above thoughts had no sooner passed through my mind, when the sergeant instructor gave the order for the students to take their machines off their stands simultaneously. I must admit, my interest was piqued, as I doubted the W.P.C. would be capable of getting her motorcycle off its stand. Well, I was proved wrong and had to eat humble pie, although as soon as the machine was standing on its two wheels unaided, I noticed she was in difficulty. On getting it off its main stand, she had inadvertently lost its centre of gravity and balance, allowing the motorcycle's weight to fall slightly away from her. The W.P.C. momentarily struggled trying to keep the BMW upright but, owing to its weight, failed miserably. She 'dropped' the motorcycle onto its offside to the concrete floor and followed it down, lying prone across the fuel tank. After it hit the deck with a load metallic bang, all went deathly quiet and the atmosphere was that thick it could have been cut with a knife. Having some sympathy with those present and not wishing to heap any further embarrassment on anyone, I made a discrete but hasty 'exit left'. I hate to say that 'I told you so', but I subsequently found out that this woman traffic officer failed her Standard Motorcycle Course and left Traffic Division to return to normal relief duties shortly afterwards. I believe there was one valuable lesson to be learnt from a case of this nature and that was, that while doing everything possible to ensure equal rights and opportunity were afforded, common sense also has to be an integral part in any selection process to guarantee quality and accuracy.

(B). I.R.A. BOMB – CANARY WHARF, DOCKLANDS – 1996

On the 6th February 1996 the I.R.A. detonated a lorry bomb at South Quay, Canary Wharf, one of the financial centres in the United Kingdom. Surveying the scene was tantamount to witnessing the apocalypse. It was truly remarkable that only two lives were lost to this incident, which devastated a great swathe of commercial property within a good half-mile radius. At the seat of the bomb was a massive crater measuring about 30 yards by 30 yards and 30 feet deep. It buckled an overhead rail and several support pillars from the Docklands Light Railway and mangled the small shopping precinct nearby. Debris, mainly masonry and glass, was spread throughout the area for a distance of at least half a mile. To my knowledge, at least two buildings, one being a Midlands Bank property built almost entirely of glass, had to be completely demolished and raised to the ground. Although costly in financial terms it was, mercifully, pretty inexpensive from a human perspective. While it really doesn't bear thinking about, had the bomb exploded half an hour earlier than it did, this country would probably have been faced with the most horrendous loss of life since the Second World War.

Shortly after the explosion occurred and the dust was beginning to settle, I arrived at the scene to assess the situation. Most of my Territorial Support Group and Traffic Division officers were already in situ, engaged in setting up cordons for safety purposes and the preservation of potential evidence. Irrespective of the fact that there were many senior personnel present from the other emergency services and Local Authority, it has always been acknowledged that the senior police officer at the scene of a major incident was in overall charge and responsible for the co-ordination and implementation of the 'clean up' operation.

I had my work cut out for me during the week following the bomb explosion, as there was a great deal of output to be coordinated in a relatively short period of time if a reasonable degree of normality was to be restored to a busy commercial area. Owing to internal politics, differences in procedures and practices and petty jealousies amongst the hierarchy of the different emergency services, my job of co-ordinating the clear-up response was, at times, made awkward, annoying and exceedingly frustrating. However, I was generally impressed with the efforts of the multi-agency approach and firmly believe that much can be achieved in the future through mutual cooperation.

(C). MURDER OF W.P.C. NINA MACKAY BY SCHIZOPHRENIC IMMIGRANT – 1997

The 24th October 1997 will be remembered by me as the saddest and most poignant day in my police career, as it was the day when the daughter of a friend and former colleague of mine was savagely murdered by a good-for-nothing psychopathic immigrant. Nina Mackay had gone out with the rest of her colleagues to execute a warrant for breach of bail conditions. Little did she know that the subject of that warrant had a pathological hatred of police. When she gained entry into his flat and confronted him, he simply stabbed her once in the chest with a seven-inch knife; she subsequently died in hospital.

To add salt to the wound, Nina's death occurred less than a month before I was due to retire upon completion of 30 years of service. Furthermore, she was a serving officer under my command in the Territorial Support Group. To add even further complexity to the situation, when I was a young constable at Old Street Police Station,

Nina's father, Sidney Mackay was my supervisory station sergeant who took me under his wing and helped me to develop as a police officer.

In view of the fact that she was killed on duty as well as being an officer under my command, I was given responsibility for organising her 'Service' funeral. Although I had the assistance of other members of my staff to help me complete many of the necessary preparations, it proved to be a very difficult situation to deal with, especially on an emotional level. My retirement from the Metropolitan Police Service after a most enjoyable and successful 30-year career should have been a happy time of celebration. Regrettably, however, owing to Nina's untimely death, it turned out to be a rather sombre occasion.

ANALYSIS

To put my 30 years of experiences in the police service into a nutshell, it would be fair to say that I have seen some phenomenal changes in both society and the police in this country during that time. People tend to be more intolerant and impatient, more prone to resort to violence than communication and much more materialistic. In short, I have witnessed what can only be described as a gradual, yet pronounced, deterioration in the basic fabric of society. The code of conduct that I was brought up with, which includes standards, values, ethics, morals and personal discipline, has clearly taken a nose dive. I often ask myself where will it all end; I haven't a clue, but I like to remain optimistic, so maybe there is hope for future generations.

I thoroughly enjoyed my police career, as it provided me with a fascinating, absorbing, rewarding and challenging life. However, I have no regrets having left that particular rat race when I did and I certainly wouldn't be at the forefront of a queue to join the Police Service today. Like society, it has changed beyond all recognition, much of which I remain far from impressed with. The Service is now steeped in a performance culture where statistics and management theories are all important. It has become too introspective, fearing internal recriminations as well as external criticism. Unfortunately, the police by their very nature are 'damned if they do and damned if they don't'. The reduction in both financial and manpower resources, coupled with the cry for enhanced performance targets, is clearly making a 'policeman's lot' an even harder one.

In my considered opinion, I believe that the general level of service to the public has been compromised. **Gone** are the days of the 'vocational' police officer; it is now little more than any other job, a means of earning a living. I am not trying to infer that there are no committed or dedicated police officers out there, as that would be unfair and wholly inaccurate. **Gone** are the days of the experienced senior practitioner, most are now theorists, giving rise to an army of 'the blind leading the blind'. Sadly, **gone** are the days of true companionship, camaraderie and loyalty. Finally, also **gone** are the days when 'grass roots' police officers were recognised and treated as the most important part of the Service. While they may still be paid lip service, the reality is that police officers at the sharp end are now simply regarded as a commodity, to be discarded when their demagogues feel they have reached the end of their useful shelf life. For the police service to thrive, grow and prosper in the future, more effort needs to be expended in the areas of loyalty, motivation, morals and commitment.

I very much appreciate that I am 'an old-style copper from a bye-gone age' and that there will be some of my contemporaries out there who will feel my views are antiquated and obsolete and therefore irrelevant. I would simply remind them of the sentiment 'if it ain't broke, don't fix it'! Policing is all about serving the law-abiding public, enforcing the law, maintaining public tranquillity and protecting the vulnerable within society. Having been a policeman for a large part of my adult life, it has reminded me of our frailty and the need to cherish every moment we have with our families and friends, as we can never be certain what lies beyond the next bend!

POSTSCRIPT

With past generations, when 'communities' remained close together and fairly static, family histories, stories, etc. were handed down from generation to generation by word of mouth. However, with the advent of travel, improved accommodation and the growth in career opportunities, the basic fabric of the 'closed' community started to disintegrate. Consequently, it became patently clear that unless a person's experiences were recorded in print, it was highly improbable that anything about that individual's life, personality or character would ever be known or available to future generations who may be interested in their ancestry. Save to say, that unless someone is prepared to commit themselves to paper, they would simply disappear into virtual oblivion. Accordingly, if you would like the opportunity to be known to future generations of your family, then get your pen out!